JEWISH CHRISTIANS IN THE UNITED STATES

SECTS AND CULTS IN AMERICA
BIBLIOGRAPHICAL GUIDES
(General Editor: J. Gordon Melton)
(VOL. 7)

GARLAND REFERENCE LIBRARY
OF SOCIAL SCIENCE
(VOL. 306)

BIBLIOGRAPHIES ON SECTS AND CULTS
IN AMERICA
(General Editor: J. Gordon Melton)

JEWISH CHRISTIANS
IN THE UNITED STATES
A Bibliography

Karl Pruter

GARLAND PUBLISHING, INC. • NEW YORK & LONDON
1987

Library of Congress Cataloging-in-Publication Data

Pruter, Karl, 1920–
Jewish Christians in the United States.

(Sects and Cults in America. Bibliographical guides;
vol. 7) (Garland Reference Library of Social Science;
vol. 306)
Includes index.
1. Missions to Jews—United States—Bibliography.
2. Converts from Judaism—Bibliography.   3. Christianity
and other religions—Judaism—Bibliography.
4. Judaism—Relations—Christianity—Bibliography.
5. Jewish Christians—United States—Bibliography.
I. Title.   II. Series: Sects and Cults in America.
Bibliographical guides; v. 7.   III. Series: Garland
Reference Library of Social Science; v. 306.

Z7817.P88   1987   [BV2620]   016.2899   84-48881
ISBN 0-8240-8741-0 (alk. paper)

Cover design by Mary Beth Brennan

Printed on acid-free, 250-year-life paper
Manufactured in the United States of America

CONTENTS

v

INTRODUCTION

In the increasingly pluralistic religious environment of
late-twentieth century Western society, the issues raised by the
conversion of Jews to Christianity, the subject of on-going discussion and debate within the two communities, for centuries have
assumed even broader implication. The interaction of evangelical
Christianity and missionary religions with non-conversionist
faiths, the power exercised by culturally dominant (not to mention politically powerful) religious communities over minority
religious groups, and the life of converts and apostates become
intensified as new Eastern and occult religions and a revived
Evangelical community claimed the attention of significant numbers of America's young adults during the 1970s. In the midst of
the religious ferment of the 1970s, Jewish missions also experienced a revival, an important part of which was the emergence
of "Messianic Judaism." The Messianic Jews were converts to
Christianity who wished to keep their "cultural" identity as Jews
and who, in that endeavor, proceeded to create Christian congregations patterned on synagogues.

This book, however, is not so much a book about Jewish
missions, and/or Hebrew Christians, as about the literature generated by the movement and those groups and organizations which
have been largely responsible for publishing it. This
literature, much privately published and informally circulated
through the movement, has to date received but scant attention
from historians, social scientists, and religious scholars. It
is hoped that this bibliography will give interested researchers
a handle by which to approach this movement which is affecting so
many people's lives. It attempts to list, as exhaustively as
possible, the materials representative of the contemporary
Hebrew-Christian movement in North America and to provide a guide
to the missionary groups currently focusing their evangelistic
activity within America's Jewish community. The movement which
had waxed and waned in the decades prior to World War II, and
lost almost all of its denominational support, experienced a
revival in the 1950s occasioned in large part by the establishment of the State of Israel. A second period of noticeable
increase began in the 1970s when the Jews for Jesus emerged as a
vital element in the larger Jesus People Revival.

Because of the widespread support for Hebrew Christians and
Jewish missions within Evangelical Christianity, the amount of
literature covering its activities and advocating its cause is
staggering and the initial goal of providing an exhaustive listing had to be abandoned. While several libraries, such as that
at Moody Biblical Institute, have large collections of Jewish
Christian material, no attempt has been made to systematically
gather and archive it. New material continued to appear even
during the period of typing the final draft. However, this

vii

latter material added little to the content, proving to be additional examples of the types of material already listed, and gave some assurance that all of the significant material circulating in the contemporary movement had been located.

Thus, this bibliography centers upon the books, booklets, pamphlets, and tracts and periodicals actually published by the various organizations engaged in Jewish evangelism. Also included are a representative selection of (1) historical and descriptive material covering the nineteenth and early twentieth century, (2) articles supportive of Jewish missions in Evangelical Christian magazines and newspapers (the overwhelming majority of which are highly repetitious) have been cited to give some idea of their general content and coverage of the important issues in the debate over Messianic Judaism.

The bibliography has been organized around the various agencies engaged in Jewish evangelism in North America in the mid-1980s. Each agency is briefly identified and the material it has produced and circulated is listed. Most of these agencies are independent fundamentalist and/or conservative evangelical Protestant organizations. Having largely lost the support of denominational Protestantism during the decades of the mid-twentieth century, most of these organizations appeal for support directly to evangelical Christian congregations and individuals.

Section one of this guide provides an introduction and historical overview of Jewish Christianity from the first to the nineteenth centurys and a selective list of recent literature surveying the historical relations of Jews and Christians through the centuries. During the last century a major factor effecting Christian Jewish relations and providing a context for contemporary Jewish missions has been Christian Zionism, a movement of Christians in support of a Jewish Israel, the existence of which many Evangelical Christians view as a prerequisite of the second coming of Christ. Among the earliest of the Christian Zionists were, interestingly enough, the Jehovah's Witnesses.

The historical overview leads directly into the second section, a discussion of the revival of Jewish missions in the nineteenth century initiated in England by the London Society for Promoting Christianity Among the Jews, and in the United States by the American Society for Meliorating the Condition of the Jews. These two pioneering groups embodied the emerging concern among Protestants for missions and were an early integral component of the total missionary movement which led to the dramatic spread of Christianity around the world in the decades prior to World War I. By the end of the century, significant Jewish missions, supported by prominent Christian leaders, had been formed across Europe, and American denominations had added their support to an increasing number of independent groups. Such strong support for Jewish missions had been generated, at least in part, from the obvious contribution of prominent Hebrew-Christians such as theologian August Neander, musician Felix Mendelsohn, astronomer

William Hershel, and British Prime Minister Benjamin Disrali, just to name a few.

The third section introduces those few remaining denominational efforts in Jewish evangelism, and those several independent evangelism agencies which have visible denominational alignment. Special attention was devoted to Roman Catholic missionary efforts toward the Jews. During the nineteenth and early twentieth centuries, Roman Catholic attempts to spur conversions of Jews gave way to an emphasis on dialogue with the Jewish community, an effort measurably increased especially by that Church's reaction to the horrors of the Holocaust and the resulting strong statement refuting the collective Jewish culpability for Christ's death by Vatican II.

This volume pivots on section four in which those missionary agencies which have carried the Jewish missionary thrust in America during the twentieth century are covered. Included are all of the agencies which have produced a significant amount of literature. All but a few are still in existence. An initial attempt to list the individual organizations either in chronological order by the date of their appearance or by their relative impact was abandoned in favor of an alphabetical listing, which was judged to be more useful to the average person using this volume.

The fifth section is devoted to the new Messianic movement of the 1970s, beginning with the most controversial group, the Jews for Jesus. The Jews for Jesus, while wishing to keep their Jewish cultural distinctives, have been most resistant to the formation of separate Jewish Christian congregations. The other segment of the movement, to which the term "messianic" is most properly applied, has led the way in the formation of messianic synagogues.

The new messianism contributed to the production of a body of literature responsive to the obvious success of contemporary evangelical efforts within the Jewish community. Some of this literature approaches the Jews for Jesus as part of a larger young adult "cult" problem and combines an attack upon messianic Jews with a like thrust at youth-oriented alternative religions such as the International Society for Krishna Consciousness (one of the most successful groups at attracting Jewish members) and the Unification Church (one of the least successful). Other volumes approach the Jews for Jesus as just another Evangelical Christian mission. The reaction of the Jewish community to one Evangelical effort which happened to coincide with the emergence of the Jews for Jesus as a potent conversionist force, Key 73, led to the initial attempts at Jewish Evangelical Christian dialogue. That dialogue, still in a very fragile and tentative stage, may become a major fruit of the appearance of the Jews for Jesus.

A final appraisal of the movement, based upon this survey

and a broad reading of the literature, is offered in a brief closing section. No matter how one judges the validity of the attempts by Christians to convert Jews, the significance of the growing movement, and especially of the messianic phase of it, for both the Christian and Jewish communities cannot be questioned. Among Christians, the movement keeps the continuing issues of anti-Semitism, the viability of the state of Israel, culturally-exclusive forms of Christianity, and evangelical strategy before the Church. Within the Jewish community, Christian evangelism raises question of self-definition, strategy in garnering support for Israel, and the role of conversionist groups in a religiously free society. That the movement has experienced almost three decades of increasing growth suggests that its significance will also continue to increase.

A Note on Sources

Only two large collections of systematically gathered Jewish Christian literature were located in the process of compiling this bibliography. One, at Moody Biblical Institute in Chicago, has been compiled over the century as an adjunct to the academic program in Jewish evangelism offered there. It is especially strong in fundamentalist literature; many of the leaders in Jewish evangelism had direct ties to Moody.

The second collection was developed during the 1970s by the Institute for the Study of American Religion, then also located in Chicago. Recently, the Institute moved to Santa Barbara, California, and its collection, including the large selection of Jewish-Christian material, is now housed in the library of the University of California--Santa Barbara. All the material collected by the author during the course of compiling this bibliography has been deposited in the ISAR collection. Application for access to the collection should be made to: Director ISAR, Box 90709, Santa Barbara, CA 93190-0709.

Acknowledgments

This volume was begun at the suggestion of Dr. J. Gordon Melton, Director of the Institute for the Study of American Religion, with whom I coauthored a work on the Old Catholic churches of North America. Knowing my interest in Jewish Christianity, he urged me to fill in what we both recognized as an obvious gap in religious information by compiling this bibliography. He provided many suggestions and contacts from his prior survey of Jewish missionary groups in the early 1970s, a necessary element in the successful completion of this work. I also appreciate his assistance in the final editing process.

During the production of this volume, I became indebted to numerous persons, far too many to mention individually, who supplied information and copies of literature from the many mission-

ary agencies. This assistance became vital in completing the
listings and locating obscure and out-of-print items. May each
who supplied even the smallest amount of information know my
thanks.

Karl Pruter
Highlandsville, Missouri
October 1986

JEWISH CHRISTIANS
IN THE UNITED STATES

HISTORICAL AND THEOLOGICAL BACKGROUND

A. Historical Background--Jewish Christianity in the Early Church

To understand the Christian Church, one must recognize that it was Jewish from the very beginning. Jesus Christ was a Jew, he was born of Jewish parents, and he lived his entire life as a Jew in a Jewish nation. One cannot read the New Testament without realizing what this meant for Jesus. He had been taught the scriptures, brought to the temple to worship, and given the advantages of training in the synagogue. His disciples were all Jews and, after his death, almost all of his followers for the first few decades were Jewish. In the early church it was assumed that one was Jewish; the first important issue to confront the church was whether non-Jews could be members. The question was settled at the First Council of the church which met in Jerusalem in about 49 A.D.: the church was to be for both Jews and Greeks. It should be noted that the foremost Christian missionary, the Apostle Paul, ministered first to the Jew and then to the Greek.

The Judaism of Jesus' day had become somewhat static due in large part to the Sadducees who were somewhat cautious since the land was occupied by the Romans. Even the reformed party, the Pharisees, had lost much of its original vitality. But the land also abounded with Jewish sects. The Essenes offered the challenge of the mystical life while another group, under John the

Baptist, who was a cousin of Jesus', proclaimed the coming of the Jewish Messiah. John's followers, although considerable, hardly seemed to herald an important upheaval in the Roman world, yet they would provide a beginning. Still another group in the desert at Qumran followed an ascetic monastic life.

Perhaps of greater significance was Judaism's gradually increasing influence on the traditional gentile world. Wherever Jews emigrated they established synagogues for their people. These were centers for religious instruction run by the Pharisees. Many non-Jews were attracted to these places of learning, many attended regularly, and a continually growing number were converted to the faith. A person who sought answers to life's basic questions was not without choices in the Roman world. The mostly Greek philosophers offered their complex systems of metaphysics and ethics, but their appeal was primarily limited to Roman intellectuals. More numerous were the followers of the many mystery cults that flourished throughout the Middle East and even in the Eternal City itself. These ranged from the Zoroastrians, fire worshipers from Persia, to the followers of Mithra. The majority of the people in the Roman world held some kind of nominal belief in the pagan gods of Greece and Rome and in the official worship of Caesar as the Emperor god. At this time, Judaism was a proselyting religion which attracted many adherents worldwide. Many non-Jews found in Judaism elements not found elsewhere: a personal God and a devotional system which was lacking in the pagan philosophical alternatives, plus the sophistication which they found absent in the mystery cults. In an age of many gods, monotheism had appeal, although the actual presence of God was missing.

When Jesus appeared in Jewish religious life, he was received by some as the long awaited messiah, by others with skepticism, and by still others with anger. The latter saw him not as a messiah but as an impostor who would destroy the law and the prophets. This diverse response resulted from uncertainty regarding the messiah.

Some expected that he would come as a great conqueror who would drive the Romans from Israel and restore the Jewish kingdom. Others presented a different kind of messiah who would be a suffering servant. The latter was decidedly the minority view and the vast majority rejected Jesus.

Jesus Christ, accepted by some and rejected by others, was born of the lineage of David, providing that one accepts Joseph the carpenter as his natural father. The scripture says, however, that, "He was conceived by the Holy Spirit," and this is accepted by most Christians. Jesus' mother was certainly Jewish and he was reared in the Jewish faith and in the Jewish nation. In his 39th year, he went like many others to hear and see John the Baptist, who was the foremost Jewish preacher of his day and who exhorted the people to repent of their sins and to be baptized. Baptism, it must be remembered, was a Jewish custom and, in the manner of the Jews, Jesus asked John to baptize him. According to the scriptures the Holy Spirit spoke at Jesus' baptism and acknowledged Jesus as the son of God.

Jesus then went into the wilderness for 40 days to contemplate the meaning of his experience. When he emerged, he began a ministry of teaching and healing and quickly became the most popular preacher of his day. He taught in the marketplaces, in the fields, and in the synagogues. He spoke to his fellow Jews about their faith and urged them to live it, not merely to the letter, but according to the spirit. He taught them that the law required more of them than mere literal obedience. Many of those who heard him were convinced that he was more than a preacher; he was, they thought, the long awaited messiah.

Jesus aroused opposition among many of the religious leaders of the day and, even worse, he ran afoul of the Roman authorities who occupied the land. The story of his trial, crucifixion, and subsequent resurrection are well known. But it is forgotten that the first believers, the first followers, were Jewish men and women. They, like Jesus, attended the synagogue and tried annually to visit the temple at Jerusalem in order to worship. In addition, the first seven bishops of Jerusalem were Jewish believers. To the objective observer of the time, Christians were simply another Jewish sect like the Pharisees or the Essenes. The Christians thought of themselves as Jews who believed that Jesus was the messiah. Hence, the only distinctive name they had for themselves was "believers." When Saul of Tarsus became a believer, he adopted the name Paul and began a series of missionary journeys that changed the composition of the church. He traveled throughout the Roman world visiting synagogues and preaching to his fellow Jews. Whenever the Jews of a particular town rejected his preaching, Paul would preach to the gentiles. His motto was "First to the Jew and then to the Greek." Eventually so many gentiles accepted Jesus and became part of the church that a controversy ensued about whether a gentile could become a "Believer" or not. The church leaders gathered in Jerusalem and resolved the question in favor of receiving non-Jews as full members of the church.

Most Christian writers treat the Council of Jerusalem as if it resolved once and for all questions concerning the place of gentiles in the church. As in all the councils there were those who did not accept its ruling and neither Jews nor gentiles rushed to integrate their synagogues and churches. Jewish congregations, whether they were called synagogues or churches, continued to be predominantly Jewish and continued to observe Jewish religious customs. Not only did they celebrate Passover and have Seders, but they retained circumcision as well. These people were known as Nazarenes; Paul refers to them as the Judaizers. Paul dropped many Jewish practices, and he was opposed to requiring them of the gentile converts to the faith. Neither the Council of Jerusalem nor Paul's teachings settled the issue.

The destruction of Jerusalem was the primary factor in the decline of Jewish Christianity as a distinct and visible segment of the church. When they fled Jerusalem along with the other Jews, they found themselves thrown together with other Jewish sectarians. Some were absorbed by the Zadokites, the followers of Zadok who had quarreled with the Pharisees on the interpretation of the law. Others joined the Essenes and some were attracted to the Egyptian gnostic movement. The vast majority however, having been separated from their synagogues, joined congregations of the church controlled by various gentile national groups. A great number became part of the Syrian Church and by the 4th century there were almost no distinctly Jewish congregations. The church had become a gentile institution in both membership and leadership. Only the first two popes had been Jewish, Peter and Linus; and it would not be until the year 1130 A.D. that another Jew, Anacleus II, would be chosen to sit on the seat of St. Peter.

It was not until the 19th century that Jewish Christian congregations began to reemerge. The first of these was Beni Abraham in London which came about when a group of 41 Hebrew Christians felt the need to assemble as Jewish Christians. The second, which was equally important, came out of Judaism. In 1882, Rabbi Joseph Rabinowitz preached to the Jews of Bessarabia that Jesus was indeed the messiah for whom they waited. He quickly gathered many adherents who formed synagogues and called themselves Israelites of the New Covenant. Many factors contributed to the emergence of Jewish Christianity but a principal factor was the growth of a Christian Zionist movement accompanied by a theology that emphasized the prophesied events of the "end times," a theology which gained increasing support within conservative Protestantism and Adventist circles in the nineteenth century and became a cornerstone of fundamentalism in twentieth century.

A Selected List of Sources on Jewish Christian History
(For further sources, see Cohen's bibliography (9))

1. Allen, E. L. "The Jewish Christian Church in the Fourth Gospel." _Journal of Biblical Literature_ (1955) 88-92.

2. Appleman, Hyman J. _The Jew in History and Destiny_. Grand Rapids, MI: Zondervan Publishing House, 1947. 27pp.

3. Avi-Yonah, Michael. _The Jews Under Roman and Byzantine Rule_. New York: Schocken Books, 1984. 304pp.

4. Baggatti, Bellarmino. _The Church from the Circumcision_. Translated by Eugene Hoade. Jerusalem: Franciscan Print Press, 1971. 326pp.

5. Bainton, Roland H. _The Church of Our Fathers_. New York: Charles Scribner's Sons, 1944. 248pp.

6. Brandon, Samuel G. F. _The Fall of Jerusalem and the Christian Church_. London: S.P.C.K., 1951. 294pp.

7. Bromley, Geoffrey, W. "Who Says the New Testament Is Anti-Semitic?" _Christianity Today_ (March 3, 1967) 548-49.

8. Chrysostom, John. _Discourses Against Judaizing Christians_. Baltimore, MD: Catholic University Press, 1979. 299pp.

9. Cohen, Adele Naomi. _The Judean Church, Up to A.D. 70, Bibliography_. Witwatersrand, South Africa: University of Johannesburg, 1972. 96pp.

10. Danielou, Jean. _The Dead Sea Scrolls and Primitive Christianity_. Translated by Salvator Attansasia. New York: New American Library, 1958. 118pp.

11. Davies, Alan T., ed. _Anti-Semitism and the Foundations of Christianity_. New York: Paulist Press, 1979. 258pp.

12. Davies, W.D. _Christian Origins and Judaism_. Philadelphia: Westminster Press, 1962. 261pp.

13. -----. _Jewish and Pauline Studies_.
Philadelphia: Fortress Press, 1984. 432pp.

14. De Lange, N.R. _Origen and the Jews_. London:
Cambridge University Press, 1976. 240pp.

15. Dupont-Sommer, A. _The Jewish Sect of Qumran
and the Essenes_. Translated by R.D. Barnett. New
York: Macmillan, 1956. 166pp.

16. Edersheim, Alfred. _The Life and Times of
Jesus the Messiah_. Grand Rapids, MI: William B.
Eerdmans, 1984. 645pp.

17. Filson, Floyd V. _A New Testament History_.
Philadelphia: Westminster Press, 1964. 435pp.

18. Goguel, Maurice. _The Birth of Christianity_.
Translated by H.C. Snape. London: Allen and
Unwin, 1953. 153pp.

19. Gough, Michael. _The Early Christian_. New
York: Frederick A. Praeger, 1961. 268pp.

20. Guignebert, Charles. _The Jewish World in the
Time of Jesus_. New York: University Books, 1959.
288pp.

21. Hahn, Ferdinand. _The Beginnings of the Church
in the New Testament_. Translated by Ianin and Ute
Nicol. Minneapolis: Augsburg, 1970. 104pp.

22. Jocz, Jacob. _The Jewish People and Jesus
Christ_. London: S.P.C.K., 1954. 448pp.

23. Kautsky, Karl. _Foundations of Christianity_.
New York: S.A. Russell, 1953. 401pp.

24. Keith, Khodada E. _The Passover in the Time of
Christ_. 1907. 18th ed. London: Church Missions
to the Jews, 1958. 46pp.

25. Kesich, Veselin. "The Apostolic Council of
Jerusalem." _St. Vladimir's Seminary Quarterly_
(1962) 108-117.

26. Klijn, A.F. and G. J. Reinink. _Patristic
Evidence for Jewish Christian Sects_. Leiden:

Brill, 1973. 313pp.

27. Knudson, Albert C. <u>The Prophetic Movement in Israel</u>. New York: Abingdon-Cokesbury Press, 1921. 174pp.

28. Longenecker, Richard. <u>The Christology of Early Jewish Christianity</u>. Grand Rapids: Baker Book House, 1970. 178pp.

29. McLeman, J. <u>The Birth of the Christian Faith</u>. London: Oliver and Boyd, 1962. 88pp.

30. Mowry, Lucretia. <u>The Dead Sea Scrolls and the Early Church</u>. Chicago: University of Chicago Press, 1962. 259pp.

31. Odeberg, Hugo. <u>Pharisaism and Christianity</u>. Translated by J.M. Moe. St. Louis: Concordia Publishing House, 1943. 112pp.

32. Richardson, Peter. <u>Israel in the Apostolic Church</u>. Cambridge: Cambridge University Press, 1969. 257pp.

33. Sandmel, Samuel. <u>Judaism and Christian Beginnings</u>. New York: Oxford University Press, 1978. 510pp.

34. Schonfield, Hugh J. <u>The History of Jewish Christianity: From the First to the Twentieth Century</u>. London: Duckworth, 1936. 256pp.

35. Shoeps, Hans Joachim. <u>Jewish Christianity: Factional Disputes in the Early Church</u>. Philadelphia: Fortress Press, 1969. 163pp.

36. Wilken, Robert L. <u>Judaism and the Early Christian Mind</u>. New Haven: Yale University Press, 1971. 257pp.

B. Theological Background--Christian Zionism

Dozens of Christian organizations have recently been formed for the support of Israel.

These include such diverse groups as Christians United for Israel and the International Christian Embassy in Jerusalem. Neither group seeks to convert Jews to Christianity; they adhere rather to a brand of millenarianism which holds that Christ will return only after the Jews, as Jews, return to Palestine and the Temple in Jerusalem is rebuilt. Further, they see the Jews in the Old Testament light as God's chosen people. In addition, they have gathered from the Old Testament, as have many Israelis, the firm belief that Palestine, including the West Bank and the Sinai, belong to the Jews by Divine fiat.

These views are not new to Christians, for Zionism, the movement to restore a Jewish National State in Palestine, was of Christian origin. The roots of modern Zionism go back to the Reformation; it was only with reluctance that Jews began to accept Zionism late in the 19th century. The Protestant Reformation rekindled interest in the Old Testament and led to a new and different view towards the Jews. The translations of the Bible into various vernacular tongues opened the door to lay interpretation; since the Old Testament made up the larger portion of the Bible, it tended to play a larger role in Christian lay thinking in the post-Reformation period. The Jews who lived in Europe were equated with those of the Old Testament, and God's promise to the Jews that the Holy Land would be theirs forever was taken literally. Furthermore, many Protestants embraced messianism and millenarianism, believing that Christ would return only after the Jews had been restored to Palestine.

The issue of a Jewish homeland is a complex one. On one hand, some groups loved the Jews and wished to help them regain their homeland so that both Christian and Jew might await the coming of Jesus: the returning Savior to one group and the Messiah to the other. On the other hand, there were those who despised the Jews and saw the return of the Jews to Palestine as the final solution to the Jewish problem. It was this obvious desire on the part of anti-Semites to rid the continent of the Jews that delayed support for Zionism in the Jewish community. Yet the pogroms in Eastern Europe gave the Jews a pragmatic reason to consider a homeland; their theological reasons were advanced later.

After the Reformation, the Old Testament played a new role among the Christians of Europe. It not only shaped religious thinking but it became the primary source of history among the Protestant laity. Although to the secular historian Palestine may have been the home of many peoples and the Jews may appear to have been usurpers, to Protestants of the Reformation and even today, the Old Testament account gives a different picture. Only the Jews count; they are in Palestine because God has given the land to them forever. Although Protestants are followers of Jesus, the Prince of Peace, they believe that it is divinely ordained that the Jews should occupy the land and destroy the inhabitants, whether warriors, women, or children.

At the time of the Reformation, interest was revived in the learning of Hebrew and the portrayal of Old Testament events and people in art, sculpture, and literature. At this time, Zionism made its first appearance in messianic sects that were Unitarian in approach. In the 16th century, Michael Servetus and Francis Kett were burned alive for their anti-Trinitarian views. Both taught that it was essential that God's chosen people, the Jews, should be restored to Palestine. By the early 17th century, more respected voices began to say the same thing. One of these was Thomas Brightman (1562-1607) who, in his <u>Apocalypsis Apocalypseos</u>, set forth his views on Jewish restoration which found acceptance among many members of Parliament. Brightman's publication was shortly followed by a work by Sir Henry Finch in 1621 entitled <u>The World's Great Restoration or the Calling of the Jews and (with them) of all Nations and Kingdoms of the Earth, to the Faith of Jesus Christ</u>. Sir Henry Finch tried to appeal to both Jews and Christians although the Jews of the 17th century totally rejected the idea of a return to Palestine.

As the Reformation brought non-Jewish Zionism to full flower, Christian Europe began to see the Jews not as a religious group but as in the Old Testament, as a nation. Many Christians began to give their children, not the names of saints, but the names of Old Testament prophets. In 1649, British, non-Jewish Zionism took on an interesting aspect. A petition was sent to the English Government by Johanna and Ebenezer Cartwright asking that England admit Jews, and that Parliament provide Jews with transportation to Palestine if they asked for it. The Cartwrights had a Puritan concern, not for the Jews, but for what they perceived as the scriptural promise to Christians which involved the Jews. The Puritan view was that Christ would come again only when the Jews were, first, more widely dispersed (hence the petition to admit Jews to England) and second, be restored to their homeland in Palestine.

The first Jewish interest in this line of Christian thought was shown by Manasseh ben Israel, the Chief Rabbi of Amsterdam. In his book, <u>The Hope of Israel</u>, he reiterated the Christian idea that Jews should be admitted to England, if only that they might also be restored to Palestine. Thus began an alliance of Christian and Jewish Zionism in England that continues even today. In 1655, Oliver Cromwell called the Whitehall Conference to discuss the question of the readmission of Jews to England. Rabbi Manasseh ben Israel presented his case and Cromwell gave his whole-hearted support. While this took place in England, various millenarian sects were teaching that Christ would soon come, and almost all of the sects insisted that his return would be preceded by the restoration of the Jews to Palestine. The continent was flooded with writers who urged not only that the Jews be restored to Palestine, but that Europe embark on a crusade to liberate the land from the Turks so that the Jews could establish their kingdom.

By the 19th century both Jewish and non-Jewish Zionism had a firm foundation. The most important and ardent non-Jewish Zionist of this time was Lord Anthony Ashley Cooper, the seventh

13

Earl of Shaftesbury (1801-1885). In 1839, he published an article in the <u>Quarterly Review</u> which set forth his ideas concerning Jewish restoration. His ideas were based primarily on the belief that Christ would not return until the Jews were restored to Palestine. He believed that Jews were a separate race and that only in Palestine could they find a home where they would not be aliens. Like many Zionists, he viewed Palestine as a vast wasteland waiting to be populated. It is easy to see how this argument would have appealed not only to those who cared about the Jews, but also to those who hated the Jews and sought an excuse to get rid of them. Both sides claimed that if Palestine was the true home of the Jewish people, it would be a service to them to insist upon their return. Because of this ambiguity in non-Jewish Zionism many Jews were reluctant to embrace Zionists' ideas.

Likewise, Jews did not respond to Napoleon Bonaparte's attempt to use them when he occupied Palestine. Napoleon issued a call for the Jews to return because he needed non-Turks in the area who would look to him for support. The French were only the first to perceive the usefulness of Zionism for imperial policy. Lord Palmerston embraced the same idea when Britain became interested in the area; he declared that Britain was the protector of the Jews in Palestine. From Palmerston's point of view, the greater the Jewish population, the more allies Britain would have in the region. Of course, this non-Jewish Zionism, while political in origin, was frequently couched in religious terms. To the Christians, it was offered as a fulfillment of their millennial expectations, and to the Jews, as a return to the one place in the world to which they had a rightful historic claim.

It is not surprising that voices in the Jewish community eventually arose in favor of Zionism. Yet it was not until Theodore Herzl and Chaim Weizmann took up the cause that the Jewish community began to respond. In his booklet, <u>The Jewish State</u> (1896), Herzl based his arguments on the Old Testament prophecies. To Jew and Christian alike, the argument had the force of divine imperative. With the support of the Jewish community, these men sought out prominent British statesmen like Lloyd George to support the Zionist cause. It must be pointed out that Lloyd George was an exceptional case as he had been preconditioned to Zionism through his Scottish Presbyterian heritage. Familiar with the Old Testament, he could quote to Weizman chapter and verse regarding God's promise to the Jews that Palestine would forever be their home. On November 2, 1917, the Balfour Declaration, named after Lord Arthur Balfour, stated England's support for the Jewish state. Balfour, himself, was a problematic Zionist; he showed concern when the Jews were persecuted in Eastern Europe, but was opposed to further Jewish immigration to England. Many Jews saw him as an anti-Semite who used the Jewish settlement of Palestine as an answer to "the Jewish question." Also apparent were Balfour's political motives in attempting to mobilize Jewish support for Britain's war against Germany and Turkey, her ally in the Middle East.

Finally, the Nazi holocaust convinced millions of Jews of the necessity of a Jewish homeland. Both Jews and non-Jews realized that extreme measures had to be taken to insure that the holocaust could not be repeated. The idea of a separate homeland was an idea whose time had come, but one which was supported by centuries of non-Jewish Zionist teaching. Many places might have served as a refuge, but only Palestine had the support of history and the Old Testament. Uganda was suggested and many saw America as a place of refuge. But America, like other nations, was reluctant to take all the Jews that fled the Nazi holocaust. The U.S. turned boat people away pleading that the quota was filled and salving its conscience by favoring the Zionist cause. The boat people were sent to Palestine, for the British had given Palestine to the Jews in the Balfour Declaration and the Old Testament had given the Jews title to the land. Both those who favored the Jews and those who were anti-Semitic could join in the cry, "Palestine for the Jews," or its reverse, "Jews to Palestine."

Today there are nearly 100 non-Jewish organizations for the support of Israel. These
groups are comprised mostly of conservative
Protestants who feel that we are living in the
"end times" and who await the restoration of the
Jews to Palestine and the rebuilding of the
Temple in Jerusalem. They do not expect the Jews
to be converted before the restoration, but
believe that Christ will return to begin his
earthly rule when most of the Jews are once again
in the Holy Land and the temple has been rebuilt.
These groups support Israel by sending funds for
relief, lobbying for Israeli causes, and supporting additional arms for Israel. Some groups,
like Christians United for Israel, even supported
the Israeli invasion of Lebanon. Another example
is the International Christian Embassy in
Jerusalem which supports Israel with prayer in-
tercession and relief programs for both Jews and
Arabs and which brings Christians to Israel to
help celebrate the Feast of the Tabernacle.

Across the U.S. groups like the Christians
United for Israel are meeting. They are often
fundamental and sometimes charismatic. Their
typical gospel hymns are often set to Israeli
music and are called, "Jewish Gospel Music."
Jews are seldom in attendance although they occasionally appear on the program. The intention
is not to convert Jews but rather to educate
Christians concerning Palestine and its place in
the end times. These groups interpret events in
the Middle East as certain signs that the restoration of the Jews is in its final stages and
that the Biblical prophecies regarding the end
times are about to be fulfilled. They believe
that support for Israel is not a political concern but one required of all Christians by divine
mandate. Zionism not only has Christian roots,
but most of its advocates today, as in the past,
are Christian.

General Sources on Contemporary Christian Zionism
(a Selected List)

37. Armstrong, Herbert W. <u>The United States and
Britain in Prophecy</u>. Worldwide Church of God,

1967. 192pp.

38. Barsoum, F. _Coming Mideast Wars in Prophecy_. Dallas: International Bible Association, 1980. 248pp.

39. Bloomfield, Arthur E. _Before the Last Battle, Armegeddon_. Minneapolis, MN: Bethany Fellowship, 1971. 192pp.

40. Boyd, Frank M. _Ages and Dispensations_. Springfield, MO: Gospel Publishing House, n.d. 191pp.

41. Bradbury, John W., ed. _Israel's Restoration_. New York: The Iverson-Ford Associates, n.d. 191pp.

42. Davis, George T.B. _Rebuilding Palestine According to Prophecy_. Philadelphia: Million Testaments Campaigns, 1935. 128pp.

43. -----. _Seeing Prophecy Fulfilled in Palestine_. Philadelphia: Million Testaments Campaigns, 1937. 118pp.

44. DeHaan, Richard W. _Israel and the Nations in Prophecy_. Grand Rapids, MI: Zondervan Publishing House, 1968. 146pp.

45. Dugger, Andrew N. _The Rebirth of Israel_. Jerusalem: Mt. Zion Reporter, n.d. 16pp.

46. Edersheim, Alfred. _Prophecy and History_. Grand Rapids, MI: Baker Book House, 1955. 391pp.

47. Epp, Theodore H. _God's Program for Israel_. Lincoln, NB: Back to the Bible Correspondance School, 1976. 31pp.

48. Evans, Mike. _Israel, America's Key to Survival_. Plainfield, NJ: Logos International, 1981. 252pp.

49. Graham, Bill. _Approaching Hoofbeats_. Waco, TX: Word Books, 1938. 236pp.

50. Guinness, Paul G. _Hear O Israel_. New York:

Vantage Press, 1983. 235pp.

51. Hendrikson, William. _Israel and the Bible_. Grand Rapids, MI: Baker Book House, 1968. 63pp.

52. Hudgings, Franklin. _Zionism in Prophecy_. New York: Pro-Palestine Federation of America, 1936. 64pp.

53. Hull, William L. _The Fall and Rise of Israel_. Grand Rapids, MI: Zondervan Publishing House, 1954. 424pp.

54. -----. _Israel/Key to Prophecy_. Grand Rapids, MI: Zondervan Publishing House, n.d. 104pp.

55. Hunting, Joseph H. _Israel-A Modern Miracle_. Murrumbeena, Australia: The David Press, 1969. 48pp.

56. Josephson, Elmer A. _Israel: God's Key to World Redemption_. Hillsboro, KS: Bible Light Publications, 1974. 487pp.

57. Kac, Arthur W. _The Death and Resurrection of Israel_. Baltimore: King Brothers, Inc., 1969. 239pp.

58. -----. _The Messianic Hope_. Grand Rapids, MI: Baker Book House, 1975. 353pp.

59. -----. _The Rebirth of the State of Israel_. Chicago: Moody Press, 1958. 386pp.

60. Kirban, Salem. _Countdown to Rapture_. Eugene, OR: Harvest House Publishers, 1977. 189pp.

61. -----. _Guide to Survival_. Wheaton, IL: Tyndale House Publishers, 1968. 275pp.

62. LaHaye, Tim. _The Beginning of the End_. Wheaton, IL: Tyndale House Publishers, 1972. 173pp.

63. Lambert, Lance. _The Uniqueness of Israel_. Eastbourne, G.B.: Kingsway Publications, 1980. 266pp.

64. Levitt, Zola. _Israel in Agony_. Irvine, CA:
Harvest House Publishers, 1975. 100pp.

65. Lightle, Steve. _Exodus II, Let My People Go_.
Kingswood, TX: Hunter Books, 1983. 286pp.

66. Lindsey, Hal. _The Liberation of Planet Earth_.
Grand Rapids, MI: Zondervan Publishing House,
1974. 236pp.

67. -----. _The 1980's Countdown to Armageddon_.
New York: Bantam Books, 1981. 178pp.

68. -----. _The Promise_. Irvine, CA: Harvest House
Publishers, 1982. 93pp.

69. -----. _There's A New World Coming: Prophetic
Odyssey_.   Ventura, CA: Vision House Publishers,
1973. 308pp.

70. -----. _The Rapture: Truth of Consequences_.
New York: Bantam Books, 1983. 176pp.

71. ----- with C. C. Carlson. _The Late Great
Planet Earth_. Grand Rapids, MI: Zondervan Publishing House, 1977. 180pp.

72. McCall, Thomas, and Zola Levitt. _The Coming
Russian Invasions of Israel_. Chicago: Moody
Press, 1976. 96pp.

73. -----. _Israel and Tomorrow's Temple_. Chicago:
Moody Press, 1973. 159pp.

74. McWhirter, James. _A World in a Country_.
Jerusalem: B.S.B.   International, 1983. 190pp.

75. Malgo, William. _1000 Years Peace?_ Hamilton,
OH: The Midnight Call, 1974. 90pp.

76. Michaelson, Arthur U. _The Jews and Palestine
in the Light of Prophecy_. Los Angeles: Jewish
Hope Publishing House, 1934. 84pp. Rev. ed.,
1939. 96pp.

77. Millhoen, Quilliam B. _Wars and Rumors of
Wars_. Fairfax, VA: King David Publishing Co.,
1983. 141pp.

78. Oldson, Arnold. <u>Inside Jerusalem/City of Destiny</u>. Glendale, CA: Regal-G/L Publications, 1968. 241pp.

79. Prince, Walter K. <u>In the Final Days</u>. Chicago: Moody Press, 1977. 192pp.

80. Rausch, David A. <u>Zionism Within Early American Fundamentalism</u>. New York: Edwin Mellen Press, 1979. 378pp.

81. Schor, Samuel. <u>The Everlasting Nation and Their Coming King</u>. London: Marshall, Morgan & Scott, Ltd., 1933. 127pp.

82. Shank, Robert. <u>Until the Coming of the Messiah and His Kingdom</u>. Springfield, MO: Westcott Publishers, 1982. 517pp.

83. Sharif, Regina. <u>Non-Jewish Zionism</u>. London: Zed Press, 1983. 144pp.

84. Taylor, Charles R. <u>Get All Excited-Jesus Is Coming Soon</u>. Redondo Beach, CA: Today in Bible Prophecy, 1974. 108pp.

85. Wolff, Richard. <u>Israel, Act III</u>. Wheaton, IL: Tyndale House Publishers, 1967. 94pp.

Articles

86. Couch, Malcom. "When Will the Jews Rebuild Their Temple?" <u>Moody Monthly</u> (December 1973) 34-35, 85-88.

87. Kelly, Ronald D. "Coming a Temple in Jerusalem?" <u>The Good News</u> (February 1985) 6-8, 24.

1. Christian Zionist Groups

Among the most important of the numerous organizations rallying support for Israel among Christians are Christians United for Israel, the

Shalom Fellowship, and the International Christian Embassy in Jerusalem. Founded in 1975 by David A. Lewis, Christians United for Israel, a branch of David A. Lewis Ministries, attempts to rally support for Israel among the nation's fundamentalist churches. Lewis speaks throughout the nation and the organization distributes the <u>Jerusalem Courier and Prophecy Digest</u>, both here and in Israel. Lewis believes that Israel is a fulfillment of prophecy and that the "end time" will come when more Jews settle in the Holy Land and the Temple rebuilt. The organization does not attempt to convert the Jews. Lewis is an effective apologist for the State of Israel and he vigorously supported Israel's intervention in Lebanon. Christians United for Israel and David A. Lewis Ministries have their headquarters in Springfield, MO.

The Shalom Fellowship was founded in 1979 by the Reverend Frank F. Eiklor to combat anti-Semitism and improve relations between Jews and Christians. Among its objectives are to spread the truth about the Holocaust and to speak out on behalf of Israel's right to exist within secure and recognized borders. Eiklor grew up in Chicago in an anti-Semitic home, but while a member of the Marine Corps in 1957, a deep religious experience led him to become active in Christians in Action International, a worldwide Christian mission. Shalom Fellowship publishes a newsletter entitled <u>The Shalom Letter</u>, and Rev. Eklor both conducts a broadcast ministry and teaches seminars. The organization is headquartered on a 50 acre estate in Keene, New Hampshire.

The International Christian Embassy Jerusalem established in 1980 is supported by 23 nations. It was organized primarily as a Christian support group for Israel; its goal is to "form a wall of prayer" around Jerusalem and Israel through intercessors worldwide. The group also provides both economic assistance, by promoting the export of Israeli products, and relief programs which help meet the social and welfare needs of Jewish, Arab and Christian people in Israel. The embassy brings Christians from all over the world to Jerusalem every September or October to celebrate Sukhot and to indicate to the Israel people that Israel is not alone. The ICEJ has given a new meaning to Zionism, offering assistance to Christians who feel called to live in Israel.

Besides the three mentioned above, note should be made of Christians Concerned for Israel, an organization headed by Franklin H. Littell, head of the religion department at Temple University and author of The Crucifixion of the Jews. It has attempted to gain support for Israel among liberal Protestant Christians.

Books

88. Lewis, David Allen. Magog 1982 Canceled. Harrison, AK: New Leaf Press, 1982. 100pp.

89. -----. Target for Terror. Springfield, MO: General Council of the Assemblies of God, 1982. 32pp.

Articles

90. Rausch, David A. "Eschatological Literature and the Jew." Jewish Frontier (February 1977).

91. -----. "True Friends: Evangelicals United for Zion." The American Zionist 68, 2 (November 1977) 20-22.

92. Spring, Beth. "Some Jews and Evangelicals Edge Closer on Israel Issue." Christianity Today (December 17, 1982) 33-34.

Periodicals

93. CCI Notebook. Christians Concerned for Israel. Temple University, Box 85, Philadelphia, PA 19122.

94. The Covenant. Christian Friends for Israel, 5860 N. Lincoln, Chicago, IL 60659.

95. Jerusalem Courier and Prophecy Digest. David

A. Lewis Ministries, 304 E. Manchester, Springfield, MO 65807

96. <u>News from Israel</u>. Box 438, West Columbia, SC 29171

97. <u>The Shalom Letter</u>. Keene, NH

98. Number not used.

2. Jehovah's Witnesses and Related Groups

David Max Eichorn's survey, <u>Evangelizing the American Jew</u>, makes no mention of the work of the Jehovah's Witnesses. Although the book is an expose of Jewish Missions, he ignores these aggressive missionaries because they believe, as taught by their first leader, Charles Taze Russell, that Jews were not subjects for conversion. The early Witnesses believed that a sign of the end of this world and the establishment of a theocratic kingdom would be the return of the Jews to the Holy Land. Both Russell and his successor, J.F. Rutherford, were ardent Zionists. For this reason and for their position against proselytizing Jews, they were well received by the Jewish community. In the early 1920s, when Russell spoke in New York, a considerable number of Jews came to listen to his support of Zionism.

In later years, both men turned away from Israel, suggesting that the coming of the Kingdom depended more upon missions of people proclaiming the Name of Jehovah than upon a small number of Jews returning to their original Zionist position and, in recent years, they have begun work in the Arab countries. In recent publications, they have even argued that modern Israel is doomed to fail because it is of human, rather than divine, origin.

There is little published material directed to the Jews from the main body of the Jehovah's Witnesses, the Watchtower Bible and Tract Society, although some of the numerous Bible Students Associations which have separated from the main branch have directed attention to the Jews. In 1942, a group of Jewish Bible Students began

publishing a magazine entitled <u>Jews in the News</u>.
In 1968, the publication was moved from Grand
Rapids, MI to Paradise, CA and its name changed
to <u>Israel Restoration News</u>. <u>The Israel Digest</u>
from Jerusalem was also published. In addition,
because so much of Witness literature has its
roots in the Old Testament, the evangelist who
goes door to door uses scriptures shared by Jews
and Gentiles. Jews who have never seen another
Christian evangelist are almost certain to have
encountered one from the Watchtower Bible and
Tract Society. The Watchtower Society is headquartered in Brooklyn, New York.

David Horowitz, head of the United Israel
Union, is one Jew who has taken notice of Pastor
Russell and the Zionist thread in Jehovah's Witness history. In the Union's periodical, <u>United
Israel Bulletin</u>, he has favorably mentioned Russell on a number of occasions. His recent book is
a compilation of materials, including many
originally published in the <u>Bulletin</u>.

Books

99. Horowitz, David. <u>Pastor Charles Taze Russell,
An Early American Christian Zionist</u>. New York:
Philosophical Library, 1986. 159pp.

100. Rutherford, Joseph Franklin, <u>Comfort to the
Jews</u>. Brooklyn, NY: Watchtower Bible and Tract
Society, 1925. 128pp

Periodicals

101. <u>Israel Restoration News</u> (formerly <u>Jews in
the News</u>). Paradise, CA.

SECTION TWO

THE MODERN REVIVAL OF JEWISH MISSIONS

During the nineteenth century, European and American Protestantism experienced a renewal of interest in missionary work. That renewal led to the formation of a host of missionary agencies, some denominationally supported, some independent, which directed attended to foreign countries as well as domestic groups felt to be in particular need of the church's ministrations. Among the earliest groups singled out and targeted for missionary work were the Jews. Beginning with the Society for Promoting Christianity Among the Jews in Great Britain and in the United States, the American Society for Meliorating the Condition of the Jews, missionary work grew over the nineteenth century. During the last half of the century, it was spurred by the increased migrations to America from Germany and Eastern Europe. As early as 1844, the American Baptist Society for Evangelizing the Jews gave direct denominational support to a Jewish mission. (The Reformed Church had given major support to the ASMCJ.) Soon, a number of the major denominations (the Evangelical Synod, the Presbyterians, and the Episcopalians) would initiate similar endeavors, while individual members of other churches would give support through the independent mission efforts. While most of the larger denominations supported Jewish missions well into the twentieth century, such missions always remained a minor concern. The lack of focus upon Jewish evangelism within organized Protestantism became a major contributing factor in the emergence of independent Jewish missionary structures.

Eichhorn (102) and Thompson (112) offer the best survey of the nineteenth century growth of Hebrew Christianity and missionary efforts to the Jews. However, no adequate history of the period has been as yet been written. Those interested in further exploration will need to read widely in the history of missions, the Jewish anti-missionary literature, and the biographical items on various outstanding Jewish Christians.

General Sources on Nineteenth Century Hebrew Christianity

102. Eichhorn, David Max. _Evangelizing the American Jew_. Middle Village, NY: Jonathan David Publishers, 1978. 210pp.

103. Einspruch, Henry. _Jewish Confessors of the Faith_. Brooklyn, NY: American Board of Missions to the Jews, 1925. 35pp.

104. Frank, Arnold. _What About the Jews_. Belfast: Graham & Hislop, 1944. 127pp.

105. -----. _Witnesses from Israel_. Edinburgh: Oliphant, Anderson & Ferrier, 1903. 118pp.

106. Gartenhaus, Jacob. _Famous Hebrew Christians_. Grand Rapids, MI: Baker Book House, 1979. 206pp.

107. _A Handbook of Foreign Missions_. London: Religious Tract Society, 1888. Pp. 303-12.

108. Littell, John S. _Some Great Christian Jews_. Keene, NH: The Author, 1913. 64pp. (Stories of Cross and Flag, No. 2)

109. Meyer, Lewis. _Eminent Hebrew Christians of the Nineteenth Century_. Edited by David A. Rausch. New York: Edwin Mellen Press, 1983. 145pp.

110. Sobel, B. Z. _Hebrew Christianity: The Thirteenth Tribe_. New York: John Wiley & Sons, 1974. 413pp.

111. Stevens, George H. _Jewish Christian Leaders_.
London: Oliophants, 1966. 92pp.

112. Thompson, A. E. _A Century of Jewish
Missions_. Chicago: F.H. Revell Company, 1902.

113. Wheatley, Joseph. _The Life and Letters of
Phoebe Palmer_. New York: W. C. Palmer, Publisher,
1876. 2 Vols.

A. The London Society for Promoting Christianity Among the Jews (London Jews Society)

The London Society for Promoting Christianity Amongst the Jews (best known as the London Jews Society) was organized in 1808 by Joseph Samuel Christian Frederick Frey, a Jewish Christian who had worked for the London Missionary Society. Frey broke with the L.M.S. in order to create a support system for converted Jews. He wanted to start boarding schools for children and a jobs program for adults since the converted Jew was often cut off from former ties and economic support. Further, he wanted the support of the established church and the London Missionary Society was made up largely of dissenting churches. The new society quickly established two congregations, one in Spitalfields and the other in Bethnel Green. The latter was known as the Episcopal Chapel and eventually became part of the established church. Because Frey was never ordained an Episcopal priest, he was never permitted to preach at the chapel.

Joseph Frey was born on September 21, 1771 in Franconia, Germany, and initiated into the Jewish faith as Joseph Levy. He was drawn to religion and became a Hebrew teacher at eighteen. Three years later he became a cantor, and one year after this, he also took on the duties of shochet, supervising ritual slaughter. He then toured western Germany and, after some time, settled in Wismar where he learned the shoemaking trade. During his three year apprenticeship, he studied the Christian faith, his interest having been aroused in it by a young man he met in a stagecoach during his tour through Germany. At his baptismal ceremony in the Lutheran church at New Brandenburg on May 8, 1798, he received his baptismal names of Christian Frederick Frey.

Like many new Christians, Frey wondered whether he was in the right branch of the church. He shortly left the Lutherans to join the United Brethren, and later attended the non-denominational Berlin Missionary Seminary. Late in his career he sought Anglican ordination but was refused. He was not until 1818 that he received ordination at the hands of the Presbyterians. Finally, in 1827, he was baptized by immersion and was a Baptist for the remainder of his life. Frey left the London Jews Society in disgrace having been accused and later admitting that he had seduced several of the converts. He sailed for America where he became the leader of a bizarre movement which dominated the Jewish Christian movement for two decades.

The London Jews Society never became a large work, although it has maintained a Christian witness to the Jews in London for almost 200 years. It is the oldest continuous missionary work among the Jews.

(For references to books and materials by Frey, see the section on the American Society for Meliorating the Condition of the Jews, below.)

114. Dunlop, John. <u>Memories of Gospel Triumphs Amongst the Jews During the Victorian Era</u>. London: S. W. Patridge & Co., 1894. 490pp.

115. Gidney, William Thomas. <u>At Home and Abroad</u>. London: Operative Jewish Converts Institution, 1900. 246pp.

116. ------. <u>The History of the London Society for the Propagation of Christianity Amongst the Jews</u>. London: London Society for the Propagation of Christianity Amongst the Jews, 1908. 672pp.

117. ------. <u>The Jews and Their Evangelism</u>.

London: Volunteer Missionary Union, 1899. 110pp.

118. -----. _Missions to Jews_. London: Operative Jewish Converts Institution, 1897. 118pp.

119. -----. _Sites and Scenes_. London: Operative Jewish Converts Institution, 1897-99. 2 Vols.

120. Norris, H. H. _The Origin, Progress, and Existing Circumstances of the London Society for Promoting Christianity Amongst the Jews: An Historical Inquiry_. London: J. Mawman, 1825. 512pp.

121. Spurgeon, Charles H. _The Restoration and Conversion of the Jews_. Pasadena, TX: Pilgrim Publications, n.d. 11pp. (Reprint of sermon originally preached in 1864.)

B. The Messianic Testimony

The Messianic Testimony was created in 1973 by the merger of two older missions to the Jews: the Mildmay Mission to the Jews and the Hebrew Christian Testimony to Israel. The Mildmay Mission to the Jews was founded by John Wilkinson in 1876. The Mission sought, in part, to provide an outlet for Protestant and Free Church bodies who did not feel free to deal with the London Jews Society (primarily a Church of England affiliate) to support Jewish missionary efforts. A Methodist who had worked with the British Jews Society for a short while, Wilkinson began his own work in the Mildmay district of North London. The Mission was not confined to London, and until the outbreak of World War II supported missionaries to Jewish communities in Eastern and Western Europe.

The Hebrew Christian Testimony to Israel was founded by David Baron, a Russian Jewish Christian who had a strict rabbinical upbringing. He emigrated to England where he was converted to Christianity and convinced that Jewish Christians of the diaspora should take the gospel to Israel. Baron's work became well known in the United States and his writings have been frequently reprinted, especially through the efforts of the

American Association for Jewish Evangelism
(recently renamed, International Ministries to
Israel). For many years Baron edited <u>The Scattered Nation</u>.

    After the two societies merged, Israel con-
tinued to be the focus of attention although more
than half of their missionaries served in Great
Britain and half were divided between South
Africa and Israel. Occasionally missionaries
were sent to other countries although never for
any great length of time.

Books

122. Baron, David. <u>Ancient Scriptures and the
Modern Jew</u>. London: Hodder & Staughton, 1900.
342pp. 5th ed., London: Morgan & Scott, 1916.
305pp. New ed. edited by Herman B. Cenz. Finlay,
OH: Durham Publishing Company, n.d. 153pp.

123. -----. <u>Anglo-Israelism and the True Story of
the "Lost" Tribes</u>. New York: Cook, n.d. 39pp.

124. -----. <u>A Divine Forecast of Jewish History</u>.
London: Morgan & Scott, n.d. 56pp.

125. -----. <u>The History of Israel</u>. London: Morgan
& Scott, 1928. 310pp.

126. -----. <u>The History of the Ten "Lost" Tribes:
Anglo Israelism Examined</u>. London: Morgan & Scott,
1915. 85pp.

127. -----. <u>Israel's Inalienable Possessions</u>.
London: Morgan & Scott, n.d. 93pp. Rept.: London:
Messianic Testimony, n.d. 32pp.

128. -----. <u>The Jewish Problem</u>. Chicago: Revell,
1891. 78pp.

129. -----. <u>Jews and Jesus</u>. Northwood, England:
The Hebrew Testimony to Israel [1979]. 62pp.

130. -----. <u>New Order of Priesthood</u>. London: J.
Nesbit, n.d. 73pp. Rept.: Findlay, OH: Dunham
Publishing Company, n.d. 63pp.

131. -----. <u>Rays of Messiah's Glory</u>. London: Hodder and Staughton, 1886. 274pp. Rept.: Grand Rapids: Zondervan Publishing Company, 1955. 174pp.

132. Number not used.

133. -----. <u>The Servant of Jehovah</u>. London: Morgan & Scott, 1922. 158pp. Rept.: New York: George H. Doran Company, 1922. 158pp. Rept. Minneapolis: James Family Publishing, 1978. 158pp.

134. -----. <u>The Shepherd of Israel and His Scattered Flock</u>. New York: Gospel Publishing House, n.d. 133pp.

135. -----. <u>Types, Psalms and Prophecies</u>. New York: American Board of Missions to the Jews, 1948. 363pp.

136. -----. <u>The Visions and Prophecies of Zechariah</u>. London: Morgan & Scott, 1918. 554pp.

137. -----. <u>What Think Ye of Christ? An Appeal to the Jews</u>. Chicago: n.d. 47pp.

138. Rothchild, Walter. <u>Can a Hebrew Also Be a Christian</u>. Jerusalem: The Author, n.d. 24pp.

139. Wilkinson, John. <u>God Answers Prayer</u>. London: Mildmay Mission to the Jews Book Store, [1902]. 93pp.

140. -----. <u>Israel, My Glory</u>. London: Mildmay Mission to the Jews, 1894. 310pp. Abrided ed. as: <u>God's Plan for the Jews</u>. London: Pater Noster Press, 1944. 124pp. Revised ed. as: <u>God's Plan for the Jew</u>. London: The Messianic Testimony, 1978. 118pp.

141. Wilkinson, Samuel Hinds. <u>British Israelism Examined</u>. London: J. Bale, Sons & Danielsson, 1923. 186pp.

142. -----. <u>The Divine Plan of the Ages Foreshadowed in the Jewish Calendar</u>. London: Mildmay Mission to the Jews, [1911]. 22pp.

143. -----. <u>The Evangelization of the Jews in Russia</u>. London: Mildmay Mission to the Jews, 1899. 23pp.

144. -----. <u>The Great Pogrom</u>. London: Mildmay Mission to the Jews, [1906]. 24pp.

145. -----. <u>In the Land of the North</u>. London: Marshall Bros., [1905]. 105pp.

146. -----. <u>The Israel Promises and their Fulfillment</u>. London: J. Bale, Sons & Danielsson, 1936. 195pp.

147. -----. <u>"Jacob's Trouble."</u> London: J. Bale, Sons & Danielsson, [1935]. 11pp.

148. -----. <u>The Life of John Wilkinson, the Jewish Missionary</u>. London: Morgan & Scott, 1908. 356pp.

149. -----, and S. Schor. <u>The Future of Jerusalem in Its Successive Phases with Regard to Present Events</u>. London: C. J. Thynne, 1918. 46pp.

Periodical

150. <u>The Messianic Witness</u>. London.

151. <u>The Scattered Nation</u>. London.

3. Other British Jewish-Evangelism Agencies

During the nineteenth century, a variety of Jewish missionary organizations, most very specialized, emerged throughout the British Isles. Their impact on the development of American organizations came primarily through the literature they published. American groups freely used the several Hebrew New Testaments developed in English, such as <u>The New Covenant in Hebrew and English</u> published by the Society for Distributing Hebrew Scriptures.

152. Bonar, Andrew Alexander. <u>Narrative of a Mission of Inquiry to the Jews from the Church of Scotland in 1839</u>. Edinburgh: Wm. White, 1843. 552pp. Rept as: <u>Narrative of a Visit to the Holy Land and Mission of Inquiry to the Jews</u>. Edinburgh: 1879. 555pp.

153. Margoliouth, Moses. <u>The Fundamental Principles of Modern Judaism Investigated</u>. London: B. Wertheim, 1843. 259pp.

154. -----. <u>The History of the Jews in Great Britain</u>. London: R. Bentley, 1851. 3 Vols.

155. -----. <u>Israel's Ordinances Examined</u>. London: B. Wertheim, 1849. 77pp.

156. -----. <u>The Jews in Great Britain</u>. London: J. Nisbet, 1846. 412pp.

157. -----. <u>The Lord's Anointed</u>. London: L Booth, 1856. 30pp.

158. -----. <u>The Lord's Prayer</u>. London: S. Bagster & Sons, [1976]. 180pp.

159. -----. <u>The Penitential Hymn of Judah and Israel After the Spirit</u>. London: Longman, Brown, Green and Longmans, 1856. 203pp.

160. -----. <u>A Pilgrimage to the Land of My Fathers</u>. London: R. Bentley, 1850. 2 Vols.

161. -----. <u>The Poetry of the Hebrew Pentateuch</u>. London: S. Bagster & Sons, 1871.

162. -----. <u>Sacred Ministrelsey</u>. London: Wertheim, Macintosh & Hunt, 1863. 50pp.

163. -----. <u>Vestiges of Genuine Freemasonry Amongst the Ruins of Asia, Africa, Etc.</u> London: R. Spencer, 1852. 55pp.

164. -----. <u>Vestiges of the Historic Anglo-Hebrews in East Anglia</u>. London: Longmans, Green, Reader 7 Dyer, 1870. 106pp.

165. <u>The New Covenant in Hebrew and English</u>.
Edgware, Middlesex, Eng.: The Society for Distributing Hebrew Scriptures, 1966.

4. The Scripture Gift Mission

Founded in 1888 by William Walters, a Christian printer from Birmingham, England, this work
has nine offices, located in: England, India,
Australia, South Africa, Ireland, New Zealand,
Canada, Zimbabwe, and the U.S. The American
branch was established in 1915 as a branch of the
London society and it remains an associate office
of the London group with its headquarters in
Philadelphia, PA.

Though the mission speaks to everyone, it
has special publications "for the Jew, the
Catholic, the skeptic, and the fear-ridden
person." (Our bibliography includes only those
works which deal with Jewish evangelism.) It
should be noted here that many fundamentalist
groups consider Jews and Catholics to be equally
lost. Jews are thought to place their faith in
the law, and Catholics, in the church. Catholics
who accept Jesus as their savior are urged to
come out of the church just as Jews are urged to
leave the synagogue.

Tracts and Booklets

(All published by the American Scripture Gift
Mission. Unless otherwise noted, no dates. No
authors noted.)

166. <u>Behold He Cometh</u>.

167. <u>How to Recognize the Messiah</u>. London:
Scripture Gift Mission.

168. <u>Israel's Faith and Hope</u>.

169. <u>Our Story in Brief</u>.

170. <u>The Prophet Like Unto Moses</u>.

171. <u>The Two Letters of the APOSTLE Peter</u>.

172. <u>What Think Ye of Christ?</u>

173. <u>The Words of Daniel the Prophet</u>.

174. <u>The Words of David the King</u>.

175. <u>The Words of Isaiah the Prophet</u>.

176. <u>The Words of the Psalmist</u>.

5. The American Society for Meliorating the Condition of the Jews (1820-1939)

Joseph Frey was received with interest and enthusiasm by many in the American Christian community. After touring the country and preaching about the need for missionary work among the Jews, he became the pastor of a Presbyterian church. In 1819, he received a letter from a Christian Jew who had been baptized in the Episcopal Jews Chapel in London, and who was working with the Moravian Brethren in Frankfort, Germany. The correspondent, John David Marc, (born David Donatty), wanted to settle German Jewish Christians in America. He was backed by Count Adalbert von der Recke, a nobleman of considerable means who belonged to the Moravian Brethren. Marc knew a number of Jews who had accepted Christ and then found themselves outcasts in the Jewish community and uncomfortable in the gentile Christian world. He believed that, in a small farming community in America, they would be able to live their new faith with fellow believers of similar culture and ethnic background.

After considerable correspondence, Frey was convinced that Marc's idea had merit and took it to the Morris County Society for Promoting Learning and Religion in New Jersey. Although they attempted to get Marc to come to America to promote the idea, he preferred to assist from Europe. After some debate, a Prayer Union for Israel was organized in New York City. The Union had a stormy start in August of 1813 and was dissolved over the question of allowing females to assist in the conducting of prayer services. A second group was started in 1817 and joined, in December 1819, by Elias Boudinot, a former president of the Continental Congress (1777-1784). With Frey, he organized the American Society for Colonizing and Evangelizing the Jews. In addition to his work as a statesman, Boudinot was the author of a number of religious writings including The Star in the West, an attempt to prove that American Indians descend from the Ten Lost Tribes.

In attempting to incorporate this new society, Boudinot and Frey ran into opposition in the New York State Legislature. They were told that proselyting of citizens is prohibited by the constitution. Consequently, they decided to limit their work, at least for the moment, to the resettlement of European Jewish Christians. Their new group, the American Society for Meliorating the Condition of the Jews, was incorporated and accepted on April 14, 1820 by the State of New York.

The Society began its work at Count Von der Recke's estate in Duesseldorf in the Rhine Valley where Jewish Christians were trained to become farmers before settling in America. In January 1822, the first immigrant, David Christian Jadownicky, arrived in New York. Like many who trained at Duesseldorf, Jadownicky completed his college education in America and enrolled in a seminary. He never settled on the land and, after a quarrel with the ASMCJ, left the organization to work as a missionary in Jerusalem.

Information on the Society can be found in Eichhorn (102) and Thompson (112) as well as the writings of Frey listed below. The extensive list of Frey's writings, some of which were reprinted many times, bear witness to the influence of Frey and the ASMCJ on the development of later Jewish missionary organizations in the United States.

177. Frey, Joseph Samuel Christian Frederick. <u>The</u>

Converted Jew. Boston: S. T. Armstrong, 1815. 224pp.

178. -----. A Course of Lectures on the Messiahship of Christ. New York: The Author, 1844. 300pp. Rept. as: The Messiahship of Jesus. Philadelphia: American Baptist Publication Society, 1850. 299pp.

179. -----. Essays on Christian Baptism. Boston: Lincoln & Edmunds, 1829. 123pp.

180. -----. Essays on the Passover. New York: The Author, 1834. 76pp.

181. -----. A Hebrew and English Dictionary. London: G. Wightman, 1839. 349pp.

182. -----. A Hebrew Grammar in the English Language. London: Gale, Curtis and Fenner, [1813]. 104pp. Revised ed. as: A New Edition of the Hebrew Grammar. New York: E. Bliss & E. White, 1823. 118pp.

183. -----. The Hebrew Students Pocket Companion. New York: Moore & Payne, 1835. 143pp.

184. -----. Joseph and Benjamin. New York: Moore & Payne, 1835-36. 2 Vols. 9th ed.: New York: D. Fanshaw, 1842.

185. -----. Judah and Israel. New York: D. Fanshaw, 1840.

186. -----. Narrative of J. S. C. F. Frey. London: Gale, Curtis & Fenner, 1812. 83pp. 11th ed.: New York: The Author, 1834. 176pp.

187. -----. The Object of the American Society for Meliorating the Condition of the Jews. New York: Daniel Fanshaw, 1827.

188. -----. The Scripture Types. Philadelphia: Committee on Publication [American Baptist], 1850. 2 Vols.

Periodicals

189. <u>The Hebrew Messenger</u>. New York, 1846-1847.

190. <u>The Jewish Intelligencer</u>. New York, 1836- ?

SECTION THREE

CHRISTIAN DENOMINATIONS AND JEWISH MISSIONS

A. Roman Catholic Church

     Roman Catholic efforts to evangelize the
Jews have aroused less antagonism from the traditional Jewish population than any other Christian
evangelistic effort.   As David Max Eichhorn
pointed out in _Evangelizing the American Jew_, in
recent years   Roman Catholics have not distin-
guished between Jews and other non-Catholics and,
thus, have directed only minimal specific efforts
at Jews. Among these few efforts are several
Catholic orders that were founded specifically to
convert Jews. In 1843, Father Marie Theodore
Rathisbonne founded the Congregation of Notre
Dame de Sion which soon had convents all over the
world. Over the years, however, the order has
become less interested in the conversion of Jews
than in the improvement of understanding between
Christians and Jews and the increasing of aware-
ness of the spiritual Jewish roots of
Christianity. The Congregation grew out of an ap-
parition of the Virgin Mary seen by Rathisbonne
in 1842.   In the United States, prior to World
War II the prime Jewish missionary efforts were
carried on by the Catholic Guild of Israel located in New York City; Rosalie Marie Levy, a nun
with the Daughters of St. Paul; and David
Goldstein, head of "Catholic Campaign for
Christ."

     More recently, in 1977, Father Arthur B.
Klyber incorporated the Remnant of Israel in order to bring the gospel to the Jews. Father
Klyber was converted from Orthodox Judaism while
serving in the U.S. Navy. He was ordained to the

priesthood in 1932 and has been active with the Redemptorists and in Jewish evangelism for over 50 years. Today, at age 83, he heads two important and controversial organizations. As founder and director of the Remnant of Israel, he has spoken out against the modern Roman Catholic attitude against the effort to convert Jews which is based on the two covenant theory. Fr. Klyber sees this as "red lining" the Jews out of the church. Klyber also heads Catholics United for Life, a militant pro-life group. He and some of his Jewish Christian followers regard abortion not only as immoral, but as a threat to Jews and other minorities. Citing Hitler's opposition of abortion for true Aryans and support of it for Jews, Gypsies, Poles, and other "inferior" races, Klyber's followers have used sit-ins and other non-violent means to block entrances to abortion clinics throughout the U.S. Both groups, Remnant of Israel and Catholics United for Life, are headquartered in Coarsegold, California.

A third Roman Catholic group interested in winning Jews for Christ is the Edith Stein Guild, although, like the present day Congregation of Notre Dame de Sion, it primarily stresses good relations between Christians and Jews. The Edith Stein Guild was formed in 1955 and was named in honor of a martyr of the Nazi persecutions. Edith Stein was born in a Jewish family in 1891 in Breslau and at a time when it was unusual for women to do so, she pursued a career in philosophy at Breslau and Goettingen. She was a student of the phenomenologist Edmund Husserl, and later became his assistant at Freiburg. She excelled in her field, and as a result of her studies in philosophy and in the writings of Teresa of Avila, she became interested in Christianity. She was received into the church on January 1, 1922, and asked to be admitted into the Carmelite Order. After teaching in Speyer for eight years, she began a career of writing and speaking about philosophy and pedagogy throughout Europe.

Stein became a Carmelite nun in 1933 when the Nazis were in power. When Germany became dangerous for those of Jewish background, her superiors transferred her to the Carmel of Echt, Holland. Just prior to her transfer, she completed _Finite and Eternal Being_, a major attempt to synthesize the philosophy of St. Thomas with modern thought. While in Holland, she wrote _The Science of the Cross_ which was a presentation of the life and teachings of St. John of the Cross. She was arrested with a number of priests and other religious people of Jewish origin and was executed at Auschwitz on August 10, 1942.

The Edith Stein Guild was organized as a lay Catholic organization with the following aims: (1) to extend friendship to Catholics of Hebrew heritage; (2) to foster among Catholics a better understanding of their roots in Judaism; (3) to promote a better understanding between Jews and Christians; and (4) to spread the knowledge of the life and writings of Edith Stein (Teresia Benedicta of the Cross) and to promote the cause of her beatification. The Edith Stein Guild attempts to keep before both Jew and Gentile the life of Edith Stein, a modern Jew who was received into the Roman Catholic Church. The Guild is headquartered in New York City.

The newest Roman Catholic group in the field is the Association of Hebrew Catholics, which was proposed in 1954 at a meeting in the Stella Maris Monastery in Haifa, Israel. The formal organization took place in 1979 after a controversy with the then Apostolic Delegate of Jerusalem, Msgr. Aquin Carew, over the assimilation of Jews. The issue was resolved when Msgr. Carew wrote to the AHC that "I, personally, believe we should enable them (the Jews) to accept Christ and His Church without assimilation." Fr. Elias Friedman, convener of the group, then felt authorized to launch the association and to appeal to Jews to enter the church while preserving their identity as Israelites. The organization has spread quickly and has offices in Australia, Ireland, Transvaal, and the United States. The headquarters are in Haifa, Israel.

Among the more interesting incidents in the modern, pre-Vatican II history of Roman Catholic Hebrew Christians was the conversion of Eugenio

Zolli, a rabbi in Rome, who converted during the closing months of World War II. The incident was highly publicized at the time and eventually led to a number of articles in the Jewish press and several books (220, 228).

Books

191. Bishop, Claire Huchet. How Catholics Look at Jews. New York: Paulist Press, 1974. 164pp.

192. Friedman, John. The Redemption of Israel. London: Sheed and Ward, 1947.

193. Gallery, John Ireland. Mary vs. Lucifer. Milwaukee, WI: Bruce Publishing Company, 1960. Pp.47-52.

194. Goldstein, David. Autobiography of a Campaigner for Christ. Boston: Catholic Campaigners for Christ, 1930? 416pp.

195. -----. Jewish Panorama. St. Paul: Radio Replies Press, 1940. 394pp.

196. -----. Letters Hebrew-Christian to Mr. Isaacs. St. Paul: Radio Replies Press, 1943. 298pp.

197. -----. and Martha M. Avery. Campaigning for Christ. Boston: Pilot Publishing Co., 1924. 463pp.

198. Graef, Hilda. Mystics of Our Times. Glen Rock, NJ: Paulist Press, 1963.

199. Homan, Helen Walker. Star of Jacob. New York: David McKay Company, 1953. 329pp.

200. Klyber, Arthur B. He's a Jew. Chicago: The Author, 1968, St. Alphonsus Rectory, 1969. 87pp.

201. -----. Queen of the Jews. Coarsegold, CA: Remnant of Israel, 1960. 48pp.

202. -----. Once a Jew. Chicago: The Author, 1973. 156pp.

203. -----. <u>This Jew</u>. Chicago: The Author, 1969.
124pp.

204. Lapids, Pinchas E. <u>Three Popes and the Jews</u>.
New York: Hawthorn Books, Inc., 1967. 374pp.

205. Levy, Rosalie Marie. <u>All Generations Shall
Call Me Blessed</u>. Boston: St. Paul Editions, n.d.
141pp.

206. -----. <u>Heart Talks with Jesus</u>. New York: The
Author, 1926-35. 5 Vols. Rept.: New York:
Catholic Book Publishing Company, 1944. 5 Vols.

207. -----. <u>Heart Talks with Mary</u>. New York: The
Author, 1930. 179pp. Rept.: New York: Catholic
Book Publishing Company, 1944. 2 Vols.

208. -----. <u>Heavenly Friends</u>. Boston: St. Paul
Editions, 1958. 484pp.

209. -----. <u>The Heavenly Road</u>. Baltimore: Baltimore City Ptg. & Bdg. Co., 1919. 101pp. 3rd
ed.: New York: The Author, 1923. 78pp.

210. -----. <u>Jesus the Divine Master</u>. Derby, NY:
Daughters of St. Paul, Apostalate of the Press,
[1953?]. 363pp.

211. -----. <u>Joseph the Just Man</u>. Boston: Daughters of St. Paul, 1955. 285pp.

212. -----. <u>Judaism and Catholicism</u>. New York:
The Author, 1927. 144pp.

213. -----. <u>The Man in Chains</u>. Boston: Daughters
of St. Paul, 1957. 252pp.

214. -----. <u>St. Paul, Vessel of Election</u>. Staten
Island, NY: Daughters of St. Paul, 1947. 231pp.

215. -----. <u>Thirty Years With Christ</u>. New York:
The Author, 1943.

216. -----. <u>Time to look at Love</u>. New York: The
Author, 1971. 104pp.

217. -----. <u>What Think You of Christ?</u> Boston: Daughters of St. Paul, 1962. 92pp.

218. -----, ed. <u>Why Jews Become Catholic: Authentic Narratives</u>. New York: By the Author, 1924. 206pp.

219. Number not used.

220. Newman, Louis I. <u>A "Chief Rabbi" of Rome Becomes a Catholic</u>. New York: The Renascence Press, 1945. 233pp.

221. Oesterreicher, John M. <u>Walls are Crumbling: Seven Jewish Philosophers Discover Christ</u>. New York: Devin-Adair Co., 1953. 393pp. Condensed edition as: <u>Five in Search of Wisdom</u>. Notre Dame, IN: University of Notre Dame Press, 1957. 290pp.

222. Robert, Brother. <u>The Broken Lamp</u>. Dujaric: n.p., 1957.

223. Sussman, Cornelia, and Irving Sussman. <u>The Jews and Christ</u>. Huntington, IN: Our Sunday Visitor, n.d. [1964 ?]. 117pp.

224. Teresia Renata de Spiritu Sancto, Sister. <u>Edith Stein</u>. Translated by Cecily Hastings and Donald Nicholl. London: Sheed and Ward, 1952.

225. Tomlin, E.W.F. <u>The Scholar and the Cross</u>. London: Longmans Green, 1955; and Westminster, MD: Newman Press, 1955.

226. Torres, Tereska. <u>The Converts</u>. New York: Alfred A. Knopf, 1970. 380pp.

227. Wynhoven, Peter M. H. <u>The Sincere Seekers</u>. Marrero, LA: Hope Haven Press, 1937. 361pp.

228. Zolli, Eugeno. <u>Before the Dawn</u>. New York: Sheed and Ward, 1954. 209pp.

Pamphlets and Tracts

229. Drogin, Elasah. <u>Holocaust: New and Old</u>. Coarsegold, CA: Remnant of Israel, n.d. 13pp.

Reprinted from <u>National Catholic Register</u>, September 1978.

230. <u>Edith Stein</u>. New York: Edith Stein Guild, n.d. 4pp.

231. Hanley, Boniface. <u>The Slaughter of an Innocent</u>. New York: Edith Stein Guild, 1982. 22pp.

232. Neyer, Amata. <u>A Saint for Our Times</u>. Cologne: Carmelites, n.d. 45pp.

233. Stein, Edith. <u>Reflections</u>. England: Darlington, 1979. 17pp.

234. -----. <u>Thoughts</u>. Eugene, OR: Carmelites, n.d.

235. -----. <u>Ways to Know God</u>. New York: Edith Stein Guild, 1981. 54pp.

Articles

236. "The Miraculous Conversion of Ratisbonne." <u>The Roman Catholic</u> (October 1983) 4-11.

237. Barrat, Robert. "Martyrdom of Edith Stein." <u>Commonweal</u> 55 (January 25, 1952) 396-398.

238. Bonsirvan, Joseph. "The Missionary Work of the Roman Catholic Church Among the Jews." <u>International Review of Missions</u> 25, 99 (July 1936) 354-63.

239. Brackett, S.J. "Edith Stein's Way of the Cross." <u>The Catholic World</u> 181 (May 1944) 111.

240. Braybrooke, N. "The Called and the Chosen." <u>Doctrine and Life</u> 8 (July 1958) 120-125.

241. Candish, F. "Edith Stein (1892-1942)." <u>Furrow</u> 4 (September 1953) 500-509.

242. "Catholic Jews Defend Life, Evangelization." <u>National Catholic Register</u> (September 10, 1978).

243. Collins, James. "Edith Stein and the Advance of Phenomenology." *Thought* 17 (December 1942) 685-708.

244. -----. "Review of Edith Stein's Endlishes and Ewiges Sein." *The Modern Schoolman* 29 (January 1952).

245. -----. "The Fate of Edith Stein." *Thought* 18 (June 1943) 384.

246. Devaux, Andre A. "Vocation in the Life and Thought of Edith Stein." *Philosophy Today* 2, 3/4 (Fall 1948) 172.

247. Francis, Dale. "The Gestapo's Answer." *The Voice of St. Jude* (May 1953) 11-15.

248. Gilman, Richard. "Edith Stein." *Jubilee* 3 (May 1955) 39-45.

249. Graef, Hilda C. "Edith Stein, a Carmelite Philosopher." *The Priest* 9 (November 1953) 861-868.

250. -----. "Edith Stein Contemplates the Woman of Perfection." *The Marianist* 43 (October 1957) 14-19.

251. -----. "Edith Stein and the Nazis." *The Catholic Digest* (May 1953) 48-52. Condensed from *Cross and Crown*.

252. Haines, A. "She Found Trust in God." *The Christian Family* 52 (October 1957) 12-14.

253. Holzhauer, Jean. "One in Six Million." *Commonweal* 57 (October 10, 1952) 21-23.

254. -----. "Jewess in a Gas Chamber." *Torch* 40 (March 1956) 6-8.

255. -----. "Jewish Convert." *Ave Maria* 66 (November 8, 1947) 578.

256. Klein, Charlotte. "From Conversation to Dialogue-The Sisters of Sion and the Jews: A Paradigm of Catholic-Jewish Religions?" *Journal*

of Ecumenical Studies (Summer 1981) 388.

257. Marshall, M. "Modern Martyr." Mary 19 (August 1958) 51-56.

258. Nicholl, Donald. "The Spiritual Writings of Edith Stein." Life of the Spirit 6, 65 (November 1951) 195-200.

259. Oesterreicher, John M. "Edith Stein on Womanhood." Integrity 7 (September 1953) 21-28.

260. Osterman, R. "Edith Stein, Witness to Paradox." The Catholic World 180 (March 1955) 447-451.

261. -----. "Edith Stein-Jewish Convert-Catholic Martyr." Epistle (Spring 1957).

262. Paul, L. "Martyr for the Jews." Homiletic and Pastoral Review 55 (April 1955) 577-583.

263. Przywara, Erich. "Neo-Scholasticism in Germany." The Modern Schoolman 10 (May 1933) 91-92.

264. Regnier, Margaret. "Jewish Redemptorist on the Jews." National Catholic Register (March 19, 1978).

265. Stern, K. "Dying and Yet We Live." The Catholic Worker 23 (September 1956) 3.

266. -----. "Of Rare Stature." Commonweal (December 14, 1956) 293-294.

267. Tomlin, E.W.F. "Edith Stein." Blackfriars 36 (June 1966) 216-222.

268. -----. "Edith Stein's Vocation." American Benedictine Review (Winter 1952) 348-353.

269. -----. "This is the Truth." The Sign 38 (August 1958) 45-47.

270. van Kaam, Adrian. "Jewish Convert's Feeling of Abandonment Improved Spirituality in Self and Others." The Catholic Herald Citizen (October

28, 1978.

271. Zyskowski, Bob. "This Priest is ....."   <u>The
<u>Chicago Catholic</u> 7 (October 1977) 44.

B. Lutheran Church-Missouri Synod

     One of the earliest denominational attempts
to evangelize the Jews was begun in 1883 in New
York City by the Lutheran Church-Missouri Synod.
Although missions were stoned and Christian
street preachers were beaten, the work continued
and another mission was opened in Chicago in
1942. When this mission was closed in 1956, the
denomination's evangelism to the Jews ceased.
However, in July 1977 the Convention of the
Synod decided to reopen Jewish Missions; it was
one of the few major denominations to do so in
the post-1960s period. Again the mission drew
fire, this time for reprinting some of the works
of Moishe Rosen, leader of the Jews for Jesus.
The Synod does not build separate Jewish Christian congregations, but integrates Jewish converts in established gentile congregations. The
denominational headquarters are in St. Louis,
Missouri.

272. "Missouri Synod Evangelism: Singling Out
the Jews." <u>The Christian Century</u>, (May 3, 1978).

C. Christian Reformed Church

     The Christian Reformed Church opened its
first mission to the Jews in 1913 in Paterson,
New Jersey, and five years later opened a second
one in Chciago. In 1960 the denomination closed
both missions and shifted its emphasis to improv-
ing Jewish Christian relations. The church as-
sumes that new believers will join regular Christian Reformed congregations. The Christian
Reformed Board of Home Missions has its headquarters in Grand Rapids, Michigan.

273. Huisjen, Albert. <u>Talking About Jesus with a
Jewish Neighbor</u>. Grand Rapids, MI: Christian
Reformed Board of Home Missions, n.d. 48pp. Rev.
ed.: Grand Rapids, MI: Baker Book House, 1964.
54pp.

274. -----. <u>A Guide to Christ-Centered Jewish
Evangelism</u>. Grand Rapids, MI: Baker Book House,
1966. 51pp.

D. The Committee on the Christian Approach to the
Jews of the Presbyterian Church (U.S.A.)

     The Presbyterians have been active in Jewish
missions since 1893, when the New York Presbytery
began to support the work of Herman Paul Faust at
the Allen Street Presbyterian Church. The Board
of Home Missions of the Presbyterian Church,
U.S.A. established a special Jewish department in
1908 which worked through settlement houses established in Jewish neighborhoods. In 1938 the
Presbyterian Church, U.S.A., organized the Committee on the Christian Approach to the Jews
which eventually became part of the United Presbyterian Church and then the Presbyterian Church
(U.S.A.) through a process of mergers. The committee supports one messianic congregation in
Philadelphia and the publication of a quarterly
entitled <u>Israel for Christ</u>. It devotes most of
its efforts to educating Presbyterians concerning
the Jewish roots of Christianity, and to incul-
cating a concern for Jewish neighbors. The headquarters of the Committee on the Christian Approach to the Jews is in Philadelphia, Pennsylvania.

Periodical

275. <u>Israel for Christ</u>. Philadelphia, PA

E. Baptists

Southern Baptist Convention

     Southern Baptists signaled their intentions
of at least backing away from Jewish evangelism
by discontinuing the Jewish Department of the
Home Mission Board in 1949. (See International
Board of Jewish Missions.) In spite of the low
denominational interest, individuals such as John
T. Carter and Bob Friedman, himself a converted
Jew, continue missionary activity.

276. Carter, John T. _Witness in Israel_.
Nashville: Broadman Press, 1969. 64pp.

277. Friedman, Robert. _Benjamin Alexander Sheep_.
Glendale, CA: Regal Books, 1973. 130pp.

278. -----. _If I Were a Rich Man_. San Rafael, CA:
Jews for Jesus, 1977. 14pp.

279. -----. _What's a Nice Jewish Boy Like You
Doing in the First Baptist Church_. Glendale, CA:
Regal Books, 1972. 102pp.

280. Jonas, A. Jase. _The Jewish People and the
Baptist Witness_. Atlanta, GA: Home Mission Board/
Southern Baptist Convention, n.d. 26pp.

281. Schlamm, Vera, with Bob Friedman. _Pursued_.
San Francisco: Hineni Ministries, 1972. 212pp.

282. Wishnietsky, Dan H. _Over the Stumbling
Block_. Nashville, TN: Broadman Press, 1977. 95pp.

Baptist Mid-Missions/Los Angeles Hebrew
Mission/Watchman Upon the Hills Club

     Baptist Mid-Missions, founded in 1920 as a
support organization for fundamental Baptists, is
one of the larger independent missionary
societies that has an active Jewish department.
It has an annual budget of over seven and one-
half million dollars and employs over nine

hundred workers. The Jewish department operates in ten American cities ranging from Bible study classes, telephone evangelism, support of youth camps, and correspondence Bible study. Advertisements for the latter appear in both Jewish and non-Jewish papers and periodicals. The organization is headquartered in Cleveland, Ohio under its president the Rev. C. Raymond Buck. It is an approved mission agency of the General Association of Regular Baptist Churches.

283. _Israel's Savior_. Los Angeles: Watchman Upon the Walls, n.d. 4pp.

284. _Jewish Evangelism Under Baptists Mid-Missions_. Cleveland, OH: Baptist Mid-Missions, n.d. Broadside.

285. Kurkowske, Adolph. "Surprise in the Synagogue." _The Baptist Bulletin_ (February 1969), 13-14.

286. _Ten Commandments_. Los Angeles: Watchman Upon the Walls, n.d. 20pp.

287. J.A.V. _Science Says "Finger Prints Don't Lie."_ Los Angeles: Watchman Upon the Walls, n.d. 31pp.

F. Christian and Missionary Alliance

The Christian and Missionary Alliance is a small holiness denomination created by the merger of two missionary societies in 1916. Its interest in Jewish missions began in 1920 when it opened a mission in the Times Square area of New York City. Although the denomination now has 189,000 members, the number of Jewish converts remains small, estimated at about 40 to 50 Jewish Christians. Although the New York mission is closed, Messiah's Lighthouse in Philadelphia remains as the one Jewish Christian congregation in the denomination. The Rev. Abraham Sandler reports that about 50 people attend Sunday morning services.

288. Thompson, Albert Edward. <u>The Life of A. B. Simpson</u>. Brooklyn, NY: The Christian Alliance Publishing Co., 1920. 300pp.

G. Assemblies of God

The Assemblies of God is one of the largest Pentecostal bodies which emerged from the revival of attention to the charismatic gifts of the Spirit which emerged at the beginning of the twentieth century. The General Council of the Assemblies of God was organized in 1914 at a time when most Christian denominations were eliminating their Jewish ministries. Among its founders was Louis Schneiderman, a Jewish convert. The Assemblies have shared an interest in Jewish missions throughout its years of existence. During the last two decades it has established 18 Jewish Christian congregations, and in 1983 the 12 reporting parishes claimed 3,394 members. The record of growth has been impressive: between 1978 and 1979 their missionaries established 8 new Jewish churches, synagogues, and outstations in California, Florida and Missouri. A number of journals for Jewish Christians were published beginning with the <u>Hebrew Evangel</u>, a quarterly begun in 1962. In 1966 the name was changed to <u>The Jewish Witness</u> and in 1978 it was incorporated into the <u>Assemblies of God Home Missions</u>, with the March-April issue devoted each year to Jewish missions.

The current congregations, while part of the Assemblies of God, also have membership in the Union of Messianic Jewish Congregations. They not only comprise over half of the Union's member churches, but they boast of the third largest messianic synagogue in the world. Temple Aaron Kodesh in Lauderhill, Florida is a 3,000 square foot building which has an average attendance of 165 people on Friday night and 100 people on Sunday. The Shalom Center in Chicago developed an independent publishing program in the 1970s.

289. Cohn, Leopold.   _Surprising Truths About the Nature and Doctrine of God!_ Chicago: Shalom Center, n.d. 7pp.

290. Gaon, R. _Le Chaim, To Life_. Springfield, MO: Evangelism Literature for America, 1976. 5pp.

291. -----. _So What Can I Tell You?_ Springfield, MO: Evangelism Literature for America, 1976. 5pp.

292. -----. _Who is a Jew - Really?_ Springfield, MO: Evangelism Literature for America, 1976. 5pp.

293. Glass, Arthur E. _Yeshua in the Tenanch_. Chicago: Shalom Center, n.d. 5pp.

294. Harris, Charles. _A Priority in Evangelism_. Springfield, MO: Assemblies of God, n.d. 7pp.

295. _How God Appeared to Israel_. Chicago: Jewish Friend, n.d. 5pp.

296. Hoy, Albert L. _Israel's Preparation for the Messiah_. Springfield, MO: Assemblies of God, Home Mission Department, n.d. 4pp.

297. Kalapathy, Ernest. _How a Jew May Have Peace with God_. Chicago: Shalom Center, n.d. 8pp.

298. -----. _In the Middle East Where is Jewish History Headed?_ Chicago: Shalom Center, n.d. 5pp.

299. -----. _Why Not for Jews_. Chicago: Shalom Center, n.d. 3pp.

300. -----. _Yom Kippur: Day without Atonement_. Chicago: The Hope, n.d. 3pp.

301. Keller, Felix. _A Biblical History of The Chosen People_. Springfield, MO: Gospel Publishing House, n.d. 31pp.

302. Lutzker, Marvin. _Conversion and True Jewishness_. Chicago: Shalom Center, 1965. 4pp.

303. Maffeo, Richard. _Brainwashing_. Springfield,

MO: Evangelism Literature for America, n.d. 5pp.

304. -----. Messianic Judaism. Springfield, MO:
Evangelism Literature for America, n.d. 5pp.

305. -----. Our Jewish Responsibility.
Springfield, MO: Evangelism Literature for
America, n.d. 5pp.

306. Smith, Harvey A. Study Guide to the Jewish
New Covenant. Springfield, MO: ELA, n.d. 3pp.

307. The Sound of the Shofar. Chicago: Shalom
Center, n.d. 7pp.

308. Specter, Ruth R. A Rabbi Searches the
Scriptures. Chicago: Shalom Center, n.d. 5pp.

309. Was Abraham a Jew? Chicago: Shalom Center,
n.d. 5pp.

310. What Is a True Jew? [Chicago:] n.p., n.d.
4pp.

311. Why Is a Jew? Chicago: Shalom Center, n.d.
3pp.

Periodicals

312. Hebrew Evangel. Springfield MO, 1962-1966.
Superceded by The Jewish Witness.

313. The Jewish Witness. Springfield, MO, 1966-
1978. Incorporated into Assemblies of God Home
Missions.

314. Shalom. Chicago, 1969- ?

315. Voice of the Messiah. Jewish-Christian
Fellowship, First Assembly of God, 8404 Phyllis
Place, San Diego, CA 92123.

H. The Grace Brethren Home Missions Council, Inc.

The Fellowship of Grace Brethren Churches, a

denomination of less than 35,000 members, has been active in Jewish work for more than 30 years. Their headquarters are in Winona Lake, Indiana. They maintain the Grace Brethren Messianic Testimony in Los Angeles which directs converts to area Grace Brethren Churches. No estimate regarding the number of converts is given. The January 22, 1972 issue of <u>Brethren Missionary Herald</u> featured the Jewish mission.

315a. Fraser, Isobel. "Take Heed." <u>Brethren Missionary Herald</u> (January 22, 1972). 7.

316. McClain, Alva J. <u>Daniel's Problem of the 70 Weeks</u>. Grand Rapids: Zondervan Publishing House, 1940. Rept.: 1960 73pp.

317. -----. <u>The Jewish Problem and Its Divine Solution</u>. Winona Lake, IN: BMH Books, 1972. 31pp

318. Neely, John S. "Close, But Not Good Enough." <u>Brethren Missionary Herald</u> (January 22, 1972) 4-5.

319. Pifer, Lester S. "Are You Concerned That the Jew Be Saved." <u>Brethren Missionary Herald</u> (January 22, 1972) 11.

320. Smelser, Gerald V. "A Tribute to the Jewish People." <u>Brethren Missionary Herald</u> (January 22, 1972) 8-10.

I. Seventh-Day Adventists Church/Israelite Heritage Institute

The Israelite Heritage Institute was founded by Seventh-Day Adventists who seek to bring Jews into their established congregations. Since its founding in 1845, the Seventh-Day Adventists church has actively engaged in evangelism among the Jews. From 1906 to 1916, Jewish Christian Fred C. Gilbert conducted a mission to Jews in Boston and was later appointed international field secretary. The Adventists share many dietary laws and the observance of the Sabbath with the Jews. Because of this common heritage, Seventh-Day Adventist missionaries feel that Jews should be more receptive to their preaching than to the preaching of other evangelists. The Israelite Heritage Institute has its headquarters in Newbury Park, California.

321. Gilbert, F. C. _The Cure for Crime_. Washington, DC: Review and Herald Publishing Company, 1926. 128pp.

322. -----. _Divine Predictions of Mrs. Ellen G. White Fulfilled_. South Lancaster, MA: Good Tidings Press, 1922. 464pp.

323. -----. _The Jewish Problem_. Takoma Park, MD: Review and Herald Publishing Company, 1942. 191pp.

324. -----. _From Judaism to Christianity_. Concord, MA: Good Tidings, 1911. 384pp.

325. -----. _Judaism & Christianity_. Takoma Park, MD: Review and Herald Publishing Company, 1940. 188pp.

326. -----. _Messiah in His Sanctuary_. Takoma Park, MD: Review and Herald Publishing Comapany, 1937. 248pp.

327. -----. _Practical Lessons from the Experience of Israel_. South Lancaster, MA: South Lancaster Publishing Co., 1902. 390pp.

328. Jacobson, Samuel S. _The Quest of a Jew_. Washington, DC: Review and Herald Publishing Association, 1973. 32 pp.

J. Catholic Church of God

Founded in 1956 by the Most Reverend Stephen A. Kochones, the Catholic Church of God is an attempt to incorporate elements of Messianic Judaism, Pentacostalism and Catholicism in one communion. According to Bishop Kochones, one-third of the parishioners, 65 people, in the Pasadena parish are Jewish Christians. Church headquarters are in Pasadena, California.

K. Miscellaneous Denominational Materials Concerning Jewish-Evangelism

329. Bevan, Edwyn. "Considerations on a Complaint Regarding Christian Propaganda Among Jews." _International Review of Missions_ 22, 88 (October 1933) 470-80.

330. _The Christian Approach to the Jew_. London: Edinburgh House Press, 1927. 208pp. (Report of a major interdenominational conference.)

331. "Christian Literature for the Jews." _International Review of Missions_ 5, 19 (July 1916) 474-81.

332. Hoffman, Conrad. "Modern Jewry and the Christian Church. _International Review of Missions_ 23, 90 (April 1934) 189-204.

333. Homrighausen, E. G. "Evangelism and the Jewish People." _International Review of Missions_ 39, 155 (July 1950) 318-29.

334. Kosmala, Hans. "Problems of the Hebrew Christian Church." _International Review of Missions_ 26, 101 (January 1937) 107-18.

335. Scott, Delaware W. _Christianity and the Jew_. Cincinnati, OH: Standard Publishing Company, 1914. 100pp.

336. Williams, A. Lukyn. "On Winning Jews to Jesus Christ." _International Review of Missions_ 20, 78 (April 1933) 202-09.

L. A Note on the Church of Jesus Christ of Latter-Day Saints

The Church of Jesus Christ of Latter-Day Saints is among the most aggressive evangelistic movements of the twentieth century. While not specifically targeting Jewish communities, they have welcomed converts into their fellowship. Two pamphlets (337, 339) demonstrate the Mormon appeal to Jews. In the mid-1980s, the church's plans to build the Brigham Young University Student Center in Jerusalem led to major controversy. While every student at the proposed center would have to sign an agreement not to proselytize while staying there, Jewish leaders have seen it as a training ground for future Jewish missionaries. The church has reportedly developed a training manual for Jewish missions.

337. Jewish Members. _Why I Joined the Mormon Church_. Salt Lake City, UT: Church of Jesus Christ of Latter-Day Saints, n.d. 17pp.

338. "The Mayor, the Mormons, and the Battle for Mount Scopus." _The Jewish Observer_ 17, 10 (November 1985) 45-46.

339. Richards, LeGrand. _The Mormons and the Jewish People_. Salt Lake City, UT: Church of Jesus Christ of Latter-Day Saints, n.d. 19pp.

M. A Note on Jewish-Christian Dialogue

As Roman Catholics and Liberal Protestants have dropped missionary efforts toward the Jewish community, it has been replaced with attempts at dialogue. That dialogue initiated at the beginning of this century continued through the decades during periods of more or less intensity. It has been spurred in recent decades by the charges leveled against the Christian community in the now classic sociological study, _Christian Faith and Anti-Semitism_ by Charles Y. Glock and Rodney Stark (New York: Harper & Brothers, 1966) and the continuing revelations of the enormity of

the Nazi Holocaust. A bibliography representative
of this dialogue would require an additional bibliography in all likelihood longer than this one
on Jewish-Christian evangelism. It is also beyond
the scope of this present effort. However, a few
significant items are listed below for those who
might wish to explore the more contemporary
direction taken by the denominations discussed
above.

340. de Poncins, Vocomte Leon. _Judaism and the
Vatican_. London: Britons Publishing Company,
1967. 199pp.

341. Eckardt, A. Roy. _Your People, My People_. New
York: Quadrangle, 1974. 275pp.

342. Littell, Franklin. _The Crucifixion of the
Jews_. New York: Harper & Row, 1975. 153pp.

343. Schneider, Peter. _The Dialogue of Christians
and Jews_. New York: Seabury Press, 1966. 196pp.

344. Woods, James E., Jr., ed. _Jewish-Christian
Dialogue in Today's World_. Waco, TX: Baylor
University Press, 1971. 164pp.

SECTION FOUR

INDEPENDENT MISSIONARY ORGANIZATIONS

A. The American Board of Missions to the Jews

The American Board of Missions to the Jews (ABMJ) was founded in 1894 by Leopold Cohn, a rabbi who had immigrated to the U.S. from Hungary. For many years its claim to be the "biggest name in Jewish evangelism" was certainly true. It began in Brooklyn as the Brownsville Mission to the Jews. Initial support from the Home Missionary Society of the American Baptist Church which began in 1896 was dropped in 1908, and the work continued as an independent effort.

A year later Cohn opened a mission in Brooklyn which he named Beth Sar Shalom. His most effective missionary tool was the periodical, _The Chosen People_. Published on a monthly basis since 1898, it is still widely circulated among Jews and gentiles alike. By 1920 Cohn had started another publication, _Shepherd of Israel_, which began as a bilingual monthly in English and Yiddish. In 1924 the society, which was then known as the Williamsburg Mission to the Jews, officially changed its name to the American Board of Missions to the Jews. It continued to grow under the leadership of Leopold and his son, J. Hoffman Cohn, supported by fundamentalist evangelical churches. Before he died in 1937, Leopold Cohn claimed that he baptized over 1,000 Jews in the Christian faith.

By the early 1970's the American Board supported an administrative staff of over 25 in North America and had a budget of nearly two million

dollars. Although it is no longer the biggest
name in Jewish evangelism, it is certainly the
financially strongest. Prior to the 1960s, and
the growth of both the Messianic churches and Jews
for Jesus, the American Board was the unchallenged
leader. It apparently aroused the envy of other
evangelistic groups which accused it of being
uncooperative. In addition, the newer groups
regard the Board as outdated. This is due in part
to the Board's disapproval of Martin Rosen's
methods in San Francisco's Haight-Asbury district.
Although both the Board and Rosen contend that the
separation of Rosen's work, Jews for Jesus, was
carried out in a friendly manner, the fact remains
that there are now two organizations and two different approaches to Jewish evangelism.

The Board's success is difficult to measure
since, in spite of its size and resources, it seldom organizes congregations. Most of its converts
join either predominantly gentile congregations
or, with increasing frequency, one of the new Messianic congregations which are often made up of
Jewish converts. It has, however, recognized that
the average Gentile congregation does not fully
meet the needs of the Jewish convert and has established a number of fellowships within which
Jewish Christians can gather. Some of these, such
as the one in Denver, carry the name Beth Sar
Shalom, after the original fellowship in Brooklyn.
Others, such as the Aedus Center in Chicago, have
different designations. The Board has offices and
centers in cities that have large Jewish
populations, such as: New York; Reston, Virginia;
Chicago; Fort Worth; and Canoga Park, California.
It has also produced a tremendous volume of
scholarly and popular works on Jewish
Christianity. The American Board of Missions to
the Jews is presently headquartered in Englewood
Cliffs, New Jersey, and its current president is
Harold A. Sevener.

Over the years the ABMJ has been able to attract
some leading figures and able writers into its
various endeavors. Charles Lee Feinberg, longtime
professor of Old Testament at Biola University in
Los Angeles originally published many of his works
with the Board. Recently, much of his shorter

material has been published and widely distributed by Emeth Publishers of Whittier, California. More recently popular writers and ABMJ staff members Thomas McCall and Zola Levitt have assumed the role previously held by the Cohns and Feinberg as the board's most prolific authors. Both Feinberg and McCall have chaired one or more of the several prophetic congresses sponsored by the Board.

345. Cohn, Joseph Hoffman. _Beginning at Jerusalem_. New York: ABMJ, 1948. 253pp.

346. -----. _I Have Fought a Good Fight_. New York: ABMJ, 1953. 316pp.

347. -----. _A Passover Trilogy_. Brooklyn: ABMJ, n.d. 29pp.

348. -----. _What Is His Son's Name_. New York: ABMJ, n.d. 32pp.

349. -----. _Will the Church Escape the Tribulation?_ Findlay, OH: Fundamental Truth Publishing, n.d. 39pp.

350. Cohn, Leopold. _The Chosen People Question Box_. Brooklyn, NY: ABMJ, 1938. 346pp. Rev.ed. by Joseph H. Cohn. Brooklyn, NY: ABMJ, 1945.

351. -----. _A Modern Missionary to an Ancient People_. N.p.: 1908. 61pp. Rev. ed. as: _The Story of a Modern Missionary to An Ancient People_. Brooklyn, NY: N.p.: 1911. 64pp. Rept. New York: ABMJ, 1962. 63pp.

352. _Down to Throop Street_. Brooklyn: ABMJ, n.d. 27pp.

353. Einspruch, Henry. _When Jews Face Christ_. Brooklyn: ABMJ: sec. ed. 1939. 201pp.

354. Feinberg, Charles L. _Daniel, the Man and His Vision_. Chappaqua, NY: Christian Herald Books, 1981. 191pp.

355. -----, ed. _Focus on Prophecy_. Westwood, NJ: Fleming H. Revell, 1964. 254pp.

356. -----. <u>God Remembers</u>. Wheaton, IL: Van Kampen Press, 1951. 283pp. Rev. ed.: Portland, OR: Multnomah Press, 1977. 284pp. 4th rev. ed.: Portland, OR: Multnomah Press, 1979. 229pp.

357. -----. <u>Habakkuk, Zephaniah, Haggai and Malachi</u>. New York: AMBJ, 1951. 150pp.

358. -----. <u>Israel in the Spotlight</u>. New York: ABMJ, 1964. 159pp. Rev. ed.: Chicago: Moody Press, 1975. 190pp. Rev. ed. as: <u>Israel at the Center of History and Revelation</u>. Portland, OR: Multnomah Press, 1980. 240pp.

359. -----, ed. <u>Jesus, the Coming King</u>. Chicago: Moody Press, 1975. 190pp.

360. -----. <u>Joel, Amos and Obadiah</u>. New York: ABMJ, 1948. 143pp.

361. -----. <u>Jonah</u>. New York: ABMJ, 1951. 163pp.

362. -----. <u>The Minor Prophets</u>. Chicago: Moody Press, 1976. 360pp.

363. -----. <u>Premillennialism or Amillennialism</u>. Grand Rapids, MI: Zondervan Publishing House, 1936. 250pp. Rev. ed. as: <u>Millennialism, the Two Major Views</u>. Chicago: Moody Press, 1980. 372pp.

364. -----, ed. <u>Prophetic Truth Unfolding Today</u>. New York: Revell, 1968. 160pp.

365. -----, ed. <u>Prophecy and the Seventies</u>. Chicago: Moody Press, 1971. 255pp.

366. -----. <u>The Prophecy of Ezekiel</u>. Chicago: Moody Press, 286pp.

367. -----. <u>Ugaritic Literature and the Book of Job</u>. Baltimore, MD: Johns Hopkins University, Ph.D. dissertation, 1945. 89pp.

368. -----. <u>Zechariah: Israels Comfort and Glory</u>. New York: ABMJ, 1952. 160pp.

369. Feinberg, John S., and Paul D. Feinberg.

Tradition and Testament. Chicago: Moody Press, 1981. 325pp. Essays in honor of Charles Lee Feinberg.

370. Fix, Janet, and Zola Levitt. For Singles Only. Old Tappan, NJ: Revell, 1978. 126pp.

371. Fruchtenbaum, Arnold. Hebrew Christianity, Its Theology, History and Philosophy. Washington, DC: Canon Press, 1974. 139pp.

372. -----. Jesus Was a Jew. Nashville: Broadman Press, 1975. 156pp.

373. Fuchs, Daniel. How to Reach the Jew for Christ. New York: ABMJ, 1943. 116pp.

374. -----. Is the Modern State, Israel, A Fulfillment of Prophecy? Englewood Cliffs, NJ: ABMJ, n.d. 27pp.

375. -----. Introducing the Jewish People to Their Messiah. Englewood Cliffs, NJ: ABMJ, 1977. 80pp.

376. Heikkila, R. Gary, and Zola Levitt. Furnace of Affliction. Harrison, AK: New Leaf Press, 1976. 124pp.

377. Heydt, Henry J. Studies in Jewish Evangelism. New York: ABMJ, 1951. 237pp.

378. -----. Introducing the Jewish People to Their Messiah. Englewood Cliffs, NJ: ABMJ, 1977. 80pp.

379. Levitt, Zola. Cairo Connection. Irvine, CA: Harvest House Publishers, 1978. 127pp.

380. -----. Corned Beef Knishes and Christ. Wheaton, IL: Tyndale House, 1975. 145pp. Rev. ed. as: Confessions of a Contemporary Jew. Wheaton, IL: Tyndale House, 1975. 145pp.

381. -----. Creation: A Scientist's Choice. Wheaton, IL: Victor Books, 1976. 131pp.

382. -----. Exhilaration: The Inspirational Side of Running. Wheaton, IL: Tyndale House Publishers, 1979.

383. -----. _Glory!_ Dallas: The Author, 1979. 26pp.

384. -----. _Guts, God and the Superbowl_. Grand Rapids, MI: Zondervan Publishing House, 1974. 119pp.

385. -----. _If You're There God, Show Me_. Chicago Moody Press, 1976. 63pp.

386. -----. _Israel in Agony_. Irvine, CA: Harvest House Publishers, 1975. 100pp.

387. -----. _An Israeli Love Story_. Chicago: Moody Press, 1978. 190pp.

388. -----. _Jesus--The Jew's Jew_. Carol Stream, IL: Creation House, 1973. 106pp.

389. -----. _Jews and Jesus_. Chicago: Moody Press, 1977. 159pp.

390. -----. _Meshumed!_ Chicago: Moody Press, 1979. 147pp.

391. -----. _Seven Churches_. Dallas: The Author, 1980. 19pp.

392. -----. _Some of My Best Friends Are Christians_. Glendale, CA: Regal, 1978. 127pp.

393. -----. _Somebody Called "Doc."_ Carol Stream, IL: Creation House, 1972. 164pp.

394. -----. _The Underground Church of Jerusalem_. Nashville, TN: Thomas Nelson, 1978. 166pp.

395. -----, and Daniel McGann. _How Did a Fat, Balding, Middle-Aged Jew Like You Become a Jesus Freak?_ Wheaton, IL: Tyndale House, 1974. 100pp.

396. -----, with Daniel McGann. _Christ at the Country Club_. Scottdale, PA: Herald Press, 1976. 120pp.

397. -----, with Ceil Rosen. _Kidnapped for My Faith_. Van Nuys, CA: Bible Voice, Inc., 1978. 127pp.

398. ----- and John Weldon. <u>Is There Life After Death?</u> Eugene, OR: Harvest House Publishers, 1977. 148pp.

399. McCall, Thomas S., ed. <u>Bicentennial Congress on Prophecy</u>. Chicago: Moody Press, 1976. 143pp.

400. ----- and Zola Levitt. <u>The Bible Jesus Read Is Exciting</u>. Garden City, NY: Doubleday, 1978. 213pp.

401. ----- and Zola Levitt. <u>The Coming Russian Invasion of Israel</u>. Chicago: Moody Press, 1974. 96pp.

402. ----- and Zola Levitt. <u>Once Through the New Testament</u>. Chappaqua, NY: Christian Herald Books, 1981. 153pp.

403. ----- and Zola Levitt. <u>Raptured</u>. Irvine, CA: Harvest House Publishers, 1975. 147pp.

404. ----- and Zola Levitt. <u>Satan in the Sanctuary</u>. Chicago: Moody Press, 1973. 120pp. Rept.: New York: Bantam Books, 1975. 112pp. Rev. ed. as: <u>Israel and Tomorrow's Temple</u>. Chicago: Moody Press, 1977. 159pp.

405. Martin, Norma and Zola Levitt. <u>Divorce, a Christian Dilemma</u>. Scottdale, PA: Herald Press, 1977. 158pp.

406. Mills, Sanford C. <u>A Hebrew Christian Looks at Romans</u>. Orangeburg, NY: ABMJ, 1971. 507pp.

407. Schwartz, Steve. <u>"Dear Rabbi."</u> Orangeburg, NY: Sar Shalom Publications, n.d. 44pp.

408. Sutton, Hilton and Zola Levitt. <u>The Mid-East Peace Puzzle</u>. Nashville: Sceptre, 1979. 112pp.

409. Unger, Merrill Frederick and Zola Levitt. <u>God Is Waiting to Meet You</u>. Chicago: Moody Press, 1975. 159pp.

410. Weldon, John and Zola Levitt. <u>Psychic Healing</u>. Chicago: Moody Press, 1982. 250pp.

411. ----- and Zola Levitt. <u>The Transcendental Explosion</u>. Irvine, CA: Harvest House Publishers, 1976. 218pp.

412. -----. <u>UFOs, What on Earth Is Happening?</u> Irvine, CA: Harvest House Publishers, 1975. 167pp. Rept. New York: Bantam Books, 1976. 175pp. Rev. ed. as: <u>Encounter with UFOs</u>. Irvine, CA: Harvest House Publishers, 1975.

Tracts

The American Board of Missions to the Jews (ABMJ) originally began to publish two sets of largely undated tracts. One, published under the imprint of the Board, was directed primarily to Christians with a series title of "What Every Christian Should Know about the Jews." The second, published under the imprint of Sar Shalom Publications, was entitled "What Every Jew Should Know." Over the years these tracts have been republished from the several headquarters of the board--New York City; Orangeburg, New York, and Englewood Cliffs, New Jersey. They have been continually upgraded, the most recent editions having color fronts, but keeping the same number of pages.

Those tracts which were part of those series have been indicated below by the code letter ("C" or "J") and their number in the series.

413. Abramovitch, L. <u>The Meaning of the Jewish Holy Days</u>. Englewood Cliffs, NJ: Sar Shalom Publications, n.d. 11pp. (J13)

414. -----. <u>An Open Letter to a Rabbi</u>. Brooklyn, NY: ABMJ, n.d. 23pp.

415. <u>Are You Ready?</u> New York: ABMJ, n.d. 3pp. (C33)

416. <u>An Astonishing Yom Kippur Prayer</u>. Englewood Cliffs, NJ: Sar Shalom Publications, n.d. 6pp. (J10)

417. Bauer, Charles G. <u>33 Prophecies Fulfilled in</u>

One Day. New York: Sar Shalom Publications, n.d. 12pp. Rev. ed. as: 27 Prophecies Fulfilled in One Day. Englewood Cliffs, NJ: Sar Shalom Publications, n.d. 10pp. (J9)

418. Brooks, Keith L. The Wonderful God of Israel. New York: Sar Shalom Publications, n.d. 10pp. (J17)

419. Bucalstein, Harry. So You Are an Agnostic! Englewood Cliffs, NJ: Sar Shalom Publications, n.d. 11pp. (J43)

420. Burgen, Harry. "And Also to the Greek." New York: ABMJ, n.d. 4pp. (C13)

421. Burgess, Norman E. The Greatest Jew That Ever Lived. New York: Sar Shalom Publications, n.d. 3pp.

422. Can a Jew Believe in Jesus and Still Be Jewish? Denver, CO: Beth Sar Shalom, n.d. 4pp.

423. Cohn, Joseph H. The Afikomon or: The Broken Matzo. Englewood Cliffs, NJ: Sar Shalom Publications, n.d. 7pp. (J16)

424. -----. The Colossal Error of A-Millenialism. Englewood Cliffs, NJ: ABMJ, n.d. 15pp. (C34)

425. -----. Communism, A Counterfeit Karl Marx Deceived Himself. New York: ABMJ, n.d. 19pp. (C64)

426. -----. Has the Church Robbed the Jews? New York: ABMJ, n.d. 19pp. (C45)

427. -----. I Believe in Science! New York: The Shepherd of Israel. n.d. 4pp. (J18)

428. -----. Is Israel the Church? New York: ABMJ, 1952. 15pp. (C34)

429. -----. It Was Necessary. Englewood Cliffs, NJ: ABMJ, n.d. 10pp. (C8)

430. -----. The Man From Petra. Englewood Cliffs, NJ: ABMJ, n.d. 19pp. (C65)

431. -----. <u>Personal Work Among Jews</u>. Englewood Cliffs, NJ: ABMJ, n.d. 15pp. (C28)

432. -----. <u>Three Days and Three Nights</u>. New York: ABMJ, n.d. 6pp. (C11)

433. -----. <u>To the Jew First</u>. Englewood Cliffs, NJ: ABMJ, n.d. 10pp. (C6)

434. -----. <u>To the Wild Olive Tree</u>. New York: ABMJ, n.d. 15pp. (C1)

435. -----. <u>A Tomorrow for the Jews</u>. New York: ABMJ, n.d. 15pp. (C3)

436. -----. <u>What Has the Jew Ever Done for the Gentile?</u> New York: ABMJ, n.d. 23pp. (C2)

437. -----. <u>What is a Christian?</u> Englewood Cliffs, NJ: Sar Shalom Publications, n.d. 11pp. (J1)

438. -----. <u>Who Gave Israel to the Robbers?</u> New York: Sar Shalom Publications, n.d. 8pp. (25)

439. -----. <u>Who Is the Meshumed?</u> New York: Sar Shalom Publications, n.d. 5pp. (J23)

440. -----. <u>Will the Antichrist Be a Jew?</u> New York: New York: ABMJ, n.d. 15pp. (C12)

441. Cohn, Leopold. <u>Behold the Virgin!</u> Englewood Cliffs, NJ: Sar Shalom Publications, n.d. 15pp. (J14)

442. -----. <u>Daniel's Seventy Weeks--What Do They Mean?</u> Translated and revised by Joseph Hoffman Cohn and Charles L. Feinberg. Englewood Cliffs, NJ: Sar Shalom Publications, n.d. 19pp. (J15)

443. -----. <u>Do Christians Worship Three Gods?</u> New York: Sar Shalom Publications, n.d. 23pp. (J28)

444. -----. <u>What Is the Son's Name</u>? New York: ABMJ, n.d. 30pp.

445. <u>The Confession of the Christian Jew</u>. Englewood Cliffs, NJ: Sar Shalom Publications,

n.d. 11pp. (J19)

446. Criswell, W.A. The God of Israel... and
America. Englewood Cliffs, NJ: ABMJ, 1976. 15pp.
(C1)

447. -----. Israel in the Plan of God. Englewood
Cliffs, NJ: ABMJ, n.d. 15pp. (C81)

448. -----. Israel in the Remembrance of God.
Englewood Cliffs, NJ: ABMJ, n.d. 16pp. (C76)

449. Did God Reject His Own People? Certainly
Not!...Says the Apostle Paul. Denver, CO: Beth Sar
Shalom, n.d. 4pp.

450. Do You Know the Biggest Name in Jewish
Evangelism? Orangeburg, NY: ABMJ, n.d. 6pp.

451. Feinberg, Charles L. Beginning at Jerusalem.
Englewood Cliffs, NJ: ABMJ, n.d. 14pp. (C22)

452. -----. Isaac and Ishmael. Englewood Cliffs,
NJ: ABMJ, n.d. 15pp. (C51)

453. -----. Should Christians Keep the Sabbath?
Englewood Cliffs, NJ: ABMJ, n.d. 10pp. (C30)

454. -----. Was Abraham a Jew? New York: Sar
Shalom Publications, n.d. 5pp. (J2)

455. -----. Why Did Messiah Have to Die? Englewood
Cliffs, NJ: Sar Shalom Publications, n.d. 6pp.
(J20)

456. -----. Why We Know the Bible Is the Word of
God. New York: ABMJ, n.d. 19pp. (C49)

457. Flynn, Leslie B. What the Church Owes the
Jew. Englewood Cliffs, NJ: ABMJ, n.d. 10pp. (C77)

458. Fruchtenbaum, A. Guitar Strums and Kosher
Pickles. New York: Sar Shalom Publications, n.d.
5pp.

459. -----. Jewishness and Hebrew Christianity.
Orangeburg, NY: Sar Shalom Publications, n.d. 7pp.
(J49)

460. -----. <u>The Nationality of the Antichrist</u>.
Englewood Cliffs, NJ: ABMJ, n.d. 36pp. (C84)

461. Frydland, Rachmiel. <u>I Escaped from the
Nazis</u>. Englewood Cliffs, NJ: ABMJ, n.d. 7pp. (C90)

462. -----. <u>The Six Million Tragedy</u>. Englewood
Cliffs, NJ: Sar Shalom Publications, n.d. 7pp.
(J53)

463. -----. <u>Why I Believe...</u> Orangeburg, NY: Sar
Shalom Publications, n.d. 22pp. (J54)

464. Fuchs, Daniel. <u>Are Jews Saved Just Because
They Are Jews?</u> New York: ABMJ, n.d. 7pp. (C62)

465. -----. <u>A "Benevolent Explosion"? Ecumenism</u>.
New York: ABMJ, n.d. 10pp. (C73)

466. -----. <u>The Dead in Christ</u>. Englewood Cliffs,
NJ: ABMJ, n.d. 10pp.

467. -----. <u>"Don't Trust the Tricky Missionaries."</u>
New York: Sar Shalom Publications, n.d. 11pp.
(J24)

468. -----. <u>Hooks in Thy Jaws</u>. Englewood Cliffs,
NJ: ABMJ, n.d. 6pp. (C86)

469. -----. <u>Is the Modern State, Israel, a Ful-
fillmet of Prophecy?</u> Englewood Cliffs, NJ: ABMJ,
1971. 27pp.

470. -----. <u>The Talmud</u>. Englewood Cliffs, NJ:
ABMJ, n.d. 15pp. (C72)

471. -----. <u>The Torah</u>. Englewood Cliffs, NJ:
ABMJ, 14pp. (C71)

472. Gold, Arlene. <u>I Found the Messiah</u>. New York:
Sar Shalom Publications, n.d. 7pp. (J31)

473. Gruen, Emil D. <u>Jews Are Being Saved</u>. New
York: ABMJ, n.d. 11pp. (C66)

474. Gruen, George. <u>Peace in These Times?</u>
Englewood Cliffs, NJ: Sar Shalom Publilcations,

n.d. 6pp. (J41)

475. Haberer, F.W. <u>World Wars III, IV, and V</u>.
Englewood Cliffs, NJ: ABMJ, n.d. 11pp. (C82)

476. Heydt, Henry J. <u>Jehovah's Witnesses</u>. New
York: ABMJ, n.d. 19pp. (C25)

477. <u>How a Gentile Became a Jew</u>. New York: ABMJ,
n.d. 7pp. Reprinted as: <u>Can a Gentile Become a
Jew?</u> Englewood Cliffs, NJ: Sar Shalom
Publications, n.d. 12pp. (J21)

478. <u>Is It Happening to You?</u> Englewood Cliffs,
NJ: Sar Shalom Publications, n.d. 4pp. (J29)

479. <u>The Jew</u>. Englewood Cliffs, NJ: ABMJ, n.d.
3pp. (C23)

480. Kalisky, Charles. <u>A Day but No Atonement</u>. New
York: Sar Shalom Publications, n.d. 11pp. (J27)

481. -----. <u>Who Is a Jew?</u> Englewood Cliffs, NJ:
Sar Shalom Publications, n.d. 7pp. (J30)

482. -----. <u>Why Was the Calendar Changed?</u>
Englewood Cliffs, NJ: Sar Shalom Publications,
n.d. 7pp. (J33)

483. Kimball, Earl H. <u>Of Whom Does Isaiah 53
Speak?</u> Orangeburg, NY: Sar Shalom Publications,
n.d. 4pp. (J11)

484. McCall, Thomas S. <u>The Importance of Passover</u>.
Englewood Cliffs, NJ: ABMJ, n.d. 5pp. (C83)

485. -----. <u>Provoke Them to Jealousy</u>. Englewood
Cliffs, NJ: ABMJ, n.d. 5pp. (C87)

486. -----. <u>Salvation Is of the Jews</u>. Englewood
Cliffs, NJ: Sar Shalom Publications, n.d. 6pp.
(J56)

487. Mills, Sanford C. <u>I Am Accused</u>. Englewood
Cliffs, NJ: Sar Shalom Publications, n.d. 7pp.
(J32)

488. -----. <u>A Rabbi's Prayer Unanswered?</u> Englewood

Cliffs, NJ: Sar Shalom Publications, n.d. 12pp.
(J50)

489. -----. A Rabbi's Quest. Englewood Cliffs,
NJ: Sar Shalom Publications, n.d. 12pp. (J48)

490. -----. The Virgin Birth. Englewood Cliffs,
NJ: Sar Shalom Publications, n.d. 5pp. (J22)

491. -----. Will a Jew Rule the World? New York:
ABMJ, n.d. 15pp. (C10)

492. The Ministry of Beth Sar Shalom Hebrew Christian Fellowship. N.p.: n.d. 3pp. (J52)

493. A Night to Be Remembered. Englewood Cliffs,
NJ: Sar Shalom Publications, n.d. 7pp. (J40)

494. O Jerusalem, Jerusalem. New York: ABMJ, n.d.
7pp.

495. Petrie, Arthur. How Near Is the Kingdom.
Englewood Cliffs, NJ: ABMJ, n.d. 17pp. (C44)

496. -----. Israel--Bone of Contention. Englewood
Cliffs, NJ: ABMJ, n.d. 19pp. (C48)

497. -----. Israel: Key to World Peace. Englewood
Cliffs, NJ: Sar Shalom Publications, n.d. 20pp.
(J42 and C74)

498. -----. "Of the Jews." Englewood Cliffs, NJ:
ABMJ, n.d. 15pp. (C52)

499. "The Rabbi Told Me So." New York: Sar Shalom
Publications, n.d. 7pp. (J6)

500. Rogers, W.H. The Errors of British-
Israelism. New York: ABMJ, n.d. 19pp. (C16)

501. -----. Have We Cast Away God's People?
Englewood Cliffs, NJ: ABMJ, n.d. 18pp. (C20)

502. -----. The Second Coming of Christ, Personal
and Premillennial. New York: ABMJ, n.d. 11pp.
(C27)

503. Sar Shalom Congregation. A Jewish Confession

of Faith. Englewood Cliffs, NJ: n.d. 5pp.

504. Schlissel, Steve. Is Jesus the Messiah?
Orangeburg, NY: Sar Shalom Publications, n.d. 2pp.
(J23)

505. So You Believe in the Rapture? New York:
ABMJ, n.d. 3pp. (C24)

506. Son Remember! New York: Sar Shalom
Publications, n.d. 4pp. (J4)

507. Stevens, Charles. What It Has Cost the
Church to Withhold Christ from the Jews. Englewood
Cliffs, NJ: ABMJ, n.d. 14pp. (C14)

508. Was Abraham a Jew? New York: Sar Shalom
Publications, n.d. 5pp. (J2)

509. Weston, Frank S. Pre--or Post--
Millennialism: Does It Matter? New York: ABMJ,
n.d. 19pp. (C18)

510. What Is a Christian? Who Is a...Jew?
Englewood Cliffs, NJ: ABMJ, n.d. 4pp. (C7)

511. Zimmerman, Elias. Twenty-one Questions About
the Jews. Englewood Cliffs, NJ: ABMJ, n.d. 15pp.

512. -----. Twenty-One Reasons. Orangeburg, NY:
Sar Shalom Publications, n.d. 23pp. (J3)

Periodicals

513. Chosen People. 100 Hunt Road, Orangeburg, New
York 10962.

514. The Shepherd of Israel. 100 Hunt Road,
Orangeburg, New York 10962.

B. American European Bethel Mission

   The American European Bethel Mission was
founded in 1937 by Rev. Leon I. Rosenberg and his
wife Frymet (Fanny). The Russian born and rab-
binically trained Rosenberg had converted shortly
after his marriage and soon left for Germany. He
became a missionary in Poland and eventually
founded the original Bethel Mission in Lodz,
destroyed by the Nazis after the invasion. The
Rosenbergs moved to California in 1937 and established their new headquarters of what was
originally called the Bethel Mission of Eastern
Europe. After World War II the work in Europe
expanded, and a mission to Israel has been added.
Headquarters are in Santa Barbara, California.

515. <u>The American European Bethel Mission, Inc.</u>
Los Angeles: n.d. 13pp.

516. <u>The Bethel Story</u>. Santa Barbara, CA: American
European Bethel Mission, 1982. 13pp. Rev. ed.:
1985. 13pp.

517. From Darkness to Light: <u>The Remarkable Life
Story of Mrs. Fanny Rosenberg</u>. Los Angeles: Bethel
Mission to Eastern Europe, n.d. 32pp.

518. Marcinkowsky, W. F. <u>The Essence of
Christianity</u>. Los Angeles: American European
Bethel Mission, n.d. 16pp.

519. Rosenberg, Leon I. <u>The Essence of Redemption</u>.
Los Angeles: American European Bethel Mission,
n.d. 32pp.

520. -----. <u>Evangelical Christianity and the
Jewish Question</u>. Los Angeles: American European
Bethel Mission, n.d. 32pp.

521. -----. <u>God's Days of Creation: My Answer to
the Sabbath Keeping Brethren</u>. Santa Barbara, CA:
American European Bethel Mission, n.d. 4pp.

522. -----. <u>Moses</u>. N. p.: n.d. 54pp.

523. -----. <u>The Secret of Missionary Commission</u>.

Santa Barbara, CA: American European Bethel
Mission, n.d. 4pp.

524. -----. <u>Why Did the Jewish Nation Reject Jesus
as Their Messiah?</u> Santa Barbara, CA: American
European Bethel Mission, n.d. 8pp.

525. -----. <u>The Various Manifestations of the
Deity</u>. Los Angeles: American European Bethel
Mission, 1961. 250pp.

526. <u>A. F. S. Messianic Guide for Jews and
Gentiles</u>. N.p.: n.d. 39pp.

Periodicals

527. <u>The Bethel Witness</u>. Box 30562, Santa Barbara,
CA 93130

528. <u>Prayer Letter</u>. Box 30562, Santa Barbara, CA
93130

C. American Messianic Fellowship (Chicago Hebrew
Mission)

     Beginning as the Chicago Hebrew Mission in
1889, the American Messianic Fellowship changed
its name and method of evangelism in 1953.   It
now attempts both to reach Jews on campus and to
educate the clergy and laity of established
churches about the need to reach out to the Jews.
It has always worked closely with the Moody Bible
Institute and has provided many of its Jewish
Christian students with practical training in
Jewish evangelism. As one of the oldest Jewish
Christian organizations, it has had some outstanding leaders including William E. Blackstone, an
ardent Christian Zionist, whose classic <u>Jesus Is
Coming</u> helped define both Fundamentalism and set
the fundamentalist attitude toward the Jews.   It
has a budget of over $100,000   annually and is
active in providing Bible Study courses by mail
and in distributing literature to the Jews. Its
headquarters are in Chicago, Illinois.

529. Blackstone, William E. <u>Jesus Is Coming</u>. New York: Fleming H. Revell, 1889. 96pp. Rev. ed.: 1898. 181pp. Frequently reprinted.

530. -----. <u>Palestine for the Jews</u>. Oak Park, IL: Privately printed, 1891. 23pp.

531. -----. <u>Satan : His Kingdom and Overthrow</u>. New York: Fleming H. Revell, 1900. 54pp.

532. -----. <u>The "Times of the Gentiles" and the "Time of the End."</u> New York: Privately printed, 1921. 28pp.

533. <u>Historical Sketch of the Chicago Hebrew Mission</u>. Chicago: Chicago Hebrew Mission, 1912. 49pp.

534. Lindberg, Milton. <u>Is Ours the Closing Generation of the Age?</u> 11th ed. Chicago: American Messianic Fellowship, 1968. 40pp.

535. -----. <u>Jacob's Trouble</u>. 6th ed. Chicago: American Messianic Fellowship, 1967. 30pp.

536. -----. <u>The Jews and Armageddon</u>. 11th ed. Chicago: American Messianic Fellowship, 1968. 40pp.

537. -----. <u>Jonah</u>. Chicago: American Messianic Fellowship, n.d. 32pp.

538. -----. <u>Russia in Prophecy</u>. 14th ed. Chicago: American Messianic Fellowship, 1968. 40pp.

539. -----. <u>The State of Israel and the Jews Today in the Light of Prophecy</u>. 10th ed. Chicago: American Messianic Fellowship, 1968. 65pp.

540. -----. <u>Treasures of Truth from the Jordan River</u>. Chicago: American Messianic Fellowship, 1933. 23pp.

541. -----. <u>Watchmen Upon the Walls of Jerusalem</u>. Chicago: American Messianic Fellowship, n.d. 23pp.

542. -----. <u>Witnessing to Jews</u>. Chicago: Chicago

Hebrew Mission, 1948. 95pp.

543. Ogden, H. Dayton. <u>How Is Your Relation with God?</u> Chicago: American Messianic Mission, 1970. 12pp.

544. Sutcliffe, B. B. <u>The Responsibility of the Church in Relation to Israel</u>. Chicago: Chicago Hebrew Mission, n.d. 15pp.

Tracts

545. Blackstone, William E. <u>The Heart of the Jewish Problem</u>. Chicago: Chicago Hebrew Mission, n.d. 16pp.

546. Blum, Jacob. <u>What Is a Hebrew Christian?</u> Chicago: American Messianic Fellowship, n.d. 8pp.

547. Buksbazen, Victor. <u>Why Don't the Rabbis Believe in Jesus</u>. Chicago: American Messianic Fellowship, n.d. 12pp.

548. <u>Chosen</u>. Chicago: American Messianic Fellowship, n.d. 5pp.

549. <u>A Christian Witness to the Jews</u>. Chicago: American Messianic Fellowship, n.d. 5pp.

550. Currie, William E. <u>The Revival That Is a Threat!</u> Chicago: American Messianic Fellowship, n.d. 4pp. Reprinted from <u>Voice</u> Magazine of March-April, 1976.

551. Goldberg, Louis. <u>Famished</u>. 1978.

552. -----. <u>Four Things from the Tenach that God Wants Us to Know</u>. Chicago: American Messianic Fellowship, n.d. 7pp.

553. <u>Isaiah, 53rd Chapter</u>. Chicago: American Messianic Fellowship, n.d. 5pp.

554. <u>Isaiah's Portrait of the Messiah</u>. Chicago: American Messianic Fellowship, n.d. 12pp.

555. Katzenellenbogen, P. <u>I Was Born a Jew, I'll</u>

Die a Jew. Chicago: American Messianic Fellowship, n.d. 5pp.

556. Lindberg, Milton B. The Difference Between Jews, Gentiles, and Christians. Chicago: American Messianic Fellowship, n.d. 11pp.

557. -----. The Doctrine of the Trinity Examined in the Light of the Tenach. Chicago: American Messianic Fellowship, n.d. 12pp.

558. -----. A Guest in a Palestinian Home. Chicago: American Messianic Fellowship, 1933. 23pp.

559. -----. Is the Gospel "To the Jew First?" Chicago: American Messianic Fellowship, n.d. 11pp.

560. -----. The Redeemer That Shall Come to Zion. Chicago: American Messianic Fellowship., n.d.16pp.

561. MacKinley,, Archie A. "Ye Shall Be My Witnesses." Chicago: American Messianic Fellowship, n.d. 4pp.

562. Mussen, Zella Reynolds. "Test Me Now in This," Says the Lord. Chicago: American Messianic Fellowship, n.d. 3pp.

563. Saxe, Israel. Day of Atonement But No Atonement. Chicago: American Messianic Fellowship, n.d. 5pp.

564. Wertheimer, Max. How a Rabbi Found Peace. Chicago: American Messianic Fellowship, n.d. 8pp.

Articles

565. Currie, William E. "A Century of Ministry." AMF Monthly 83, 10 (November 1978) 8-14.

Periodicals

566. AMF Monthly. 7448 N. Damen Avenue, Chicago, Illinois 60645.

D. Bible Christian Union (National Jewish Mission
and Message to Israel)

     Founded in 1904 by G.P. Rand, the Bible
Christian Union is a fundamentalist, interdenominational missionary agency directed at both
Jews and gentiles. Through its affiliates, Message to Israel, Inc. (founded in New York City by
Coulson Shepherd) and the National Jewish Mission,
it distributes literature door-to-door in Jewish
neighborhoods and conducts broadcasts in the U.S.,
Canada, and Europe. The Bible Christian Union
believes that since most European nations are
Catholic or misled by "modernism and dead
Protestantism," they, along with the Jews, are in
need of salvation. Out of a total staff of 93,
only 15 serve in North America. Most of the staff
is engaged in missionary work in countries such as
France, the Netherlands, Italy and West Germany.
The organization has a budget of nearly one million dollars and has its headquarters in Lebanon, PA.

567. _Bible Christian Union, Principle and
Practices_. Brooklyn, NY: Bible Christian Union,
n.d. 34pp.

568. Davies, W. Elwyn. _To the Urals and Beyond_.
Lebanon, PA: Bible Christian Union, [1979]. 15pp.

569. _The Jew_.

570. Raud, Elsa. _Introduction to Prophecy_.
Findlay, OH: Dunham Publishing Company, 1960.
236pp.

571. Shepherd, Coulson. _The Geneology of Israel's
Messiah_. 12pp.

572. ------. _The God of Abraham_. 15pp.

573. ------. _A Strange Paradox_. 7pp.

Periodical

574. <u>Increase</u>. Box 718, Lebanon, PA 17042

E. Biblical Research Society

The Biblical Research Society was founded in 1930 by David L. Cooper (d. 1984) in order to "give the Gospel to all Israel in this generation by means of suitable (free) literature." It published a number of undated tracts written by Cooper which were liberally distributed. Cooper also wrote and published a number of widely circulated books. O.E. Phillips, founder of the Hebrew Christian Fellowship of Philadelphia served on the staff of the society prior to the foundation of the Fellowship in 1944.

The society was located in Los Angeles for many years, but has recently moved its headquarters to Adelanto, California.

575. Cooper, David L. <u>Antichrist and the Worldwide Revival</u>. Los Angeles: Biblical Research Society, 1954. 31pp.

576. -----. <u>The Blueprint of the Times of the Gentiles</u>. Los Angeles: Biblical Research Society, n.d. 8pp.

577. -----. <u>Book Distribution of the Biblical Research Society</u>. Los Angeles: Biblical Research Society, n.d. 29pp.

578. -----. <u>The Eternal God Revealing Himself to Suffering Israel and Humanity</u>. Harrisburg, PA: Evangelical Press, 1928. 362pp. Rev. ed.: Los Angeles, CA: Biblical Research Society, 1953. 380pp.

579. -----. <u>Future Events Revealed</u>. Los Angeles: The Author, 1935. 208pp.

580. -----. <u>The God of Israel</u>. Los Angeles: Biblical Research Society, 1939. 46pp. Rev. ed.: 1943. 102pp. Rev. ed.: 1945. 134pp.

581. -----. <u>God's Torchbearers</u>. Los Angeles: CA: Biblical Research Society, 1953. 40pp.

582. -----. <u>Grand March of Empire</u>. Los Angeles: Biblical Research Society, 1955. 31pp.

583. -----. <u>History Repeating Itself</u>. Los Angeles: Biblical Research Society, n.d. 32pp.

584. -----. <u>Is the Fig Tree Cursed Forever?</u> Los Angeles: Biblical Research Society, 1951. 20pp.

585. -----. <u>Is the Jew Still First on God's Prophetic Program?</u> Los Angeles: Biblical Research Society, 1935. 36pp.

586. -----. <u>Man: His Creation, Fall, Redemption, and Glorification</u>. Los Angeles: Biblical Research Society, 1948. 131pp. Rev. ed.: 1950. 163pp.

587. -----. <u>Messiah: His Final Call to Israel</u>. Los Angeles: Biblical Research Society, 1962. 173pp.

588. -----. <u>Messiah: His First Coming Scheduled</u>. Los Angeles: Biblical Research Society, 1939. 555pp. Abridged ed.: 1939. 171pp. Rev. ed.: 1953. 571pp.

589. -----. <u>Messiah: His Glorious Appearance Imminent</u>. Los Angeles: Biblical Research Society, 1961. 203pp.

590. -----. <u>Messiah: His Historical Appearance</u>. Los Angeles: Biblical Research Society, 1958. 431pp. Abridged ed.: 1961. 200pp.

591. -----. <u>Messiah: His Nature and Person</u>. Los Angeles: The Author, 1933. 224pp. Abridged ed.: Los Angeles: The Author, 1933. 128pp.

592. -----. <u>Messiah: His Redemptive Career</u>. Los Angeles: The Author, 1932. 101pp. Rev. ed.: 1935. 134pp.

593. -----. The New Sanhedrin. Los Angeles: The Author, 1930. 79pp.

594. -----. Prophetic Fulfillments in Palestine Today. Los Angeles: Biblical Research Society, 1940. 125pp.

595. -----. The 70 Weeks of Daniel. Los Angeles: Biblical Research Society, 1941. 71pp.

596. -----. The Shepherd of Israel Seeking His Own. Los Angeles: Biblical Research Society, 1962. 165pp.

597. -----. What Men Must Believe, or God's Greatest Provision for Mankind. Los Angeles: Biblical Research Society. Abridged Edition: 1943. 208pp.

598. -----. When Gog's Armies Meet the Almighty. Los Angeles: Biblical Research Society, 1940. 112pp.

599. -----. When Will Wars Cease. Los Angeles: Biblical Research Society, 1941. 82pp.

600. -----. Who Holds the Key? Los Angeles: Biblical Research Society, n.d. 11pp.

601. -----. Why God's Interest Is in the Jew. Los Angeles: Biblical Research Society, 1941. 47pp.

602. -----. A Wise and Faithful Steward of the Lord. Los Angeles: Biblical Research Society, [1948]. 22pp.

603. -----. Why God's Interest Is in the Jew. Los Angeles: Biblical Research Society, 1941. 47pp.

604. -----. The World's Greatest Library Graphically Illustrated. Los Angeles: Biblical Research Society, 1942. 123pp.

605. Cooper, Florence Lita. A Modern Gideon and Mrs. Gideon. Los Angeles: The Author, 1942. 78pp.

606. Phillips, E. O. Birth Pangs of a New Age.

Los Angeles: Biblical Research Society, 1941.
127pp.

Tracts
(These tracts by David Cooper are all undated and
were published by the society in Los Angeles)

607. <u>First Coming of Messiah Schedules</u>

608. <u>Historical Appearance of Messiah</u>

609. <u>How May One Become Wise?</u>

610. <u>The Imminent Second Coming of Messiah</u>

611. <u>The Importance of the Literary Method</u>

612. <u>Israel, Prepare to Meet Thy God</u>

613. <u>Israel's Seven Musts and Jehovah's Seven I
Wills</u>

614. <u>Nature and Person of Messiah</u>

615. <u>Normal Christian Growth</u>

616. <u>Redemptive Career of Messiah</u>

617. <u>Some Vital Question</u>

618. <u>Spiritual Immunination</u>

619. <u>The Study of the Psalms</u>

620. <u>Things Old and New</u>

621. <u>A Thought for the New Year</u>

622. <u>The Triumph of David's Greater Son</u>

623. <u>The Triune Nature of the God of Israel</u>

624. <u>The Triune Nature of the Supreme Being</u>

625. <u>Where Some Find Peace and Joy</u>

626. <u>Wishful Thinking</u>

Periodical

627. <u>Biblical Research Monthly Magazine</u>. 19111
Panther Avenue, Adelanto, CA 92301

F. Buffalo Hebrew Mission

     The Buffalo Hebrew Mission was established in
1947 to evangelize Jews in Western and Central New
York and Northern Pennsylvania. It carries on a
diversified ministry which includes a radio
program, the "Messianic Hour," a telephone
ministry, and house to house canvassing.

628. <u>"That You May Know Our Affairs."</u> Buffalo, NY:
Buffalo Hebrew Christian Mission, n.d. 5pp.

Periodical

629. <u>Israel's Messsenger</u>. Box 1675, Buffalo, NY
14216

G. The Christian Jew Foundation

     Founded by Charles Halff in 1948, the founda-
tion sponsors a radio broadcast called the Christian Jew Hour. Beginning in Alabama on a small
250-watt station, the Christian Jew Hour is heard
on some 40 stations each day and claims to be the
largest Hebrew Christian broadcast in the world.
It begins with lively Hebrew Christian gospel
music and is followed by a sermon given by the
Rev. Charles Halff.

     Halff was born in 1928 in San Antonio, Texas,
of Jewish parents, and until he was 15 years old,
he was active in the Reformed Jewish temple. A
Christian acquaintance gave him some Christian

booklets and the New Testament to read, and on
June 30, 1943 he professed faith in Christ. His
family was disturbed and sent him to college in
Tulsa, hoping that he would return to join the
real estate business. Later, when Halff told his
father that he had decided to enter the Christian
ministry, his father had him jailed and filed an
insanity charge against him. After the court
found the charge baseless his father disowned
him. In his biography Halff states that his
grandmother offered him $85,000 to recant his
Christian faith.

     In 1947, Halff was ordained to the ministry
in a Baptist church in Tulsa and began his radio
ministry a year later. He estimates that his
broadcasts reach five million people each day and
says that he receives over 50,000 letters per
year. He claims to have written more than 50
books on Biblical subjects. The Christian Jew
Foundation is headquartered in San Antonio, Texas.

Books (All published in San Antonio by the Christian Jew Foundation unless otherwise noted.)

630. Halff, Charles. <u>Did the Jews Kill Christ?</u>

631. -----. <u>Enemies of the Christian</u>. 1966. 23pp.

632. -----. <u>The Fallacies of Easter</u>. n.d. 12pp.

633. -----. <u>The Four Baptisms</u>. 1974. 24pp.

634. -----. <u>God's Last Two Prophets</u>.

635. -----. <u>God's Predestination</u>.

636. -----. <u>Great End-Times Prophecies</u>. 1975.
58pp.

637. -----. <u>The Hebrew Passover</u>. 1964. 36pp.

638. -----. <u>How to Lead a Jew to Christ</u>. n.d.
13pp.

639. -----. <u>Israel, Egypt and the End</u>.

640. -----. <u>Israel, Nation of Destiny</u>. 1974. 26pp.

641. -----. *Israel's Place in Prophecy.*

642. -----. *Marriage, Divorce and Remarriage.*

643. -----. *The Rapture, When and How?*

644. -----. *Should the Sabbath Be Observed Today?*

645. -----. *Should We Tithe?*

646. -----. *The Truth About Christmas.* n.d. 18pp.

647. -----. *What It Costs a Jew to Become a Christian?* n.d. 64pp.

648. -----. *Where Are the Ten Lost Tribes?*

649. -----. *Why Do Christians Have to Suffer?*

650. -----. *Why Jews and Arabs Fight.*

651. -----. *Will There Be a War Between Russia and America?*

652. Kroll, Woodrow M. *Seven Bible Fools.* 1973. 35pp.

653. Linton, John. *Will Christ Come in This Generation?* 1962. 59pp.

Tracts
(All written by Charles Halff and published by the Christian Jew Hour in San Antonio, Texas.)

654. *Do You Know the Messiah?* n.d. 5pp.

655. *4 Things Every Jew Should Know.*

656. *How to Be Saved.*

657. *How to Recognize the Messiah.*

658. *Our Messiah Has Come!* n.d. 6pp.

659. *Why Am I Here?*

660. <u>Ha'OR (The Light)</u>, Box 345, San Antonio, TX 78292.

661. <u>Message of The Christian Jew</u>, Box 345, San Antonio, TX 78292.

H. Emeth Publications and Charles Feinberg

Emeth Publications is a faith ministry engaged in publishing literature concerning the gospel of salvation primarily for Jews. It has published several books and many tracts written by Dr. Charles L. Feinberg, professor of Semitics and Old Testament at Talbot Theological Seminary in LaMirada, CA. This literature is widely used by other missions to the Jews. The organization is based in Whittier, California. Feinberg's writings published elsewhere are listed under the appropriate organizations (such as the American Board of Missions to the Jews).

(All materials listed, except as noted, are by Feinberg, and all are without exception published by Emeth Publications in Whitter, California.)

662. <u>Good News for the Jews</u>. n.d. 25pp.

663. <u>Is the Virgin Birth in the Old Testament?</u> 1967. 77pp.

Tracts
(All undated)

664. <u>Barrabas or Messiah?</u> 5pp.

665. <u>Can a Jew Approach God?</u> 5pp.

666. <u>Can a Jew Believe in a God-Man?</u> 5pp.

667. <u>Can a Jew Believe in the Trinity?</u> 5pp.

668. <u>Can a Jew Believe in the Virgin Birth?</u> 5pp.

669. <u>The Curse of Anti-Semitism</u>. 15pp

670. <u>The Day of Atonement, But Where Is the Blood?</u> 5pp.

671. <u>The Feasts of Lights</u>. 5pp.

672. <u>Feast of Purim</u>. 8pp.

673. <u>The Feast of the Passover</u>. 5pp.

674. <u>4 Things God Wants the Jew to Know</u>. 7pp.

675. <u>He Shall Save His People</u>. 4pp.

676. <u>How Could Israel Recognize the Messiah?</u> 5pp.

677. <u>Ichabod Over Israel</u>. 5pp.

678. <u>Israel, the Apple of God's Eye</u>. 5pp.

679. <u>Israel's Babe of Bethlehem</u>. 5pp.

680. <u>A Kingdom of Priests and a Holy Nation</u>. 5pp.

681. <u>The Lost Sheep of Israel</u>. 5pp.

682. <u>Messiah in the Synagogue</u>. 5pp.

683. <u>Messiah the Light of the World</u>. 5pp.

684. <u>Of Whom Does the Prophet Say This?</u> 5pp.

685. <u>The Precious Christ</u>. 5pp.

686. <u>The Snare of Tradition</u>. 5pp.

687. <u>"They Murmured Because of Him."</u> 5pp.

688. <u>What Christmas Should Mean to the Jew</u>. 4pp.

689. <u>What Every Jew Needs Most</u>. 5pp.

690. <u>What the Risen Messsiah Should Mean to Israel</u>. 5pp.

691. <u>Who Crucified Jesus?</u> 5pp.

692. <u>Why Did Messiah Have to Die?</u> 5pp.

693. <u>Without Book--No Remission</u>. 5pp.

694. Feinberg, Charles L. and Anne P. Feinberg.
<u>Salvation Through Blood</u>. 5pp.

I. Friends of Israel

     Founded in 1938 to provide material and
spiritual aid for Hebrew Christians and Jews suffering from Nazi persecution, the society, under
the leadership of Dr. Victor Buksbazen, is today
working in 8 countries to evangelize the Jew.
The group is strongly opposed to the formation of
separate Jewish Christian congregations. Much of
their work consists of conducting seminars in how
to share the Christian faith with Jewish friends.
Articles in their bi-monthly magazine, <u>Israel My
Glory</u>, are often directed to gentile as well as
Jewish readers. The Friends of Israel is also
devoted to evangelism among Jewish students on
American campuses. Their literature points out
that while Jews make up about two percent of the
population in the U.S., they compose about fif-
teen percent of the college and university
community.

     The present International Director for the
organization is the Rev. Marvin J. Rosenthal. In
1975, the group had a staff of 16 and an annual
budget of over $500,000 with most of its funding
coming from fundamentalist churches. It is headquartered in West Collingswood, New Jersey.

695. Buksbazen, Lydia. <u>They Looked for a City</u>.
Philadelphia: The Friends of Israel, 1955.   2nd.
ed., 1960. 216pp.

696. Buksbazen, Victor. <u>The Feasts of Israel</u>.
Fort Washington, PA: Christian Literature
Crusade, 1954. 102pp.

697. -----. <u>The Gospel in the Feasts of Israel</u>.
Philadelphia: The Friends of Israel, The Spearhead Press, 1954. 80pp.

698. -----. <u>Isaiah Fifty-Three, Of Who Does the
Prophet Speak?</u> West Collingswood, NJ: The Friends

of Israel Gospel Ministry, 1975. 17pp.

699. -----. <u>Miriam, The Virgin of Nazareth</u>.

700. -----. <u>The Prophet Isaiah</u>.

701. McQuaid, Elwood. <u>It Is No Dream</u>. West Collingswood, NJ: The Spearhead Press, 1978. 260pp.

702. -----. <u>Zvi</u>. West Collingswood,NJ: The Spearhead Press, 1978. 202pp.

Tracts
(All published by the Friends of Israel Gospel Ministry in West Collingswood, New Jersey.)

703. Bukksbazen, Victor. <u>I Was Born a Jew and I Will Die a Jew</u>. n.d. 4pp.

704. -----. <u>Immortality in Jewish Thought</u>. n.d. 12pp.

705. -----. <u>Isaiah Fifty-three, Of Whom Does the Prophet Speak?</u> 1975. 17pp.

706. -----. <u>Rehearsal for Armegeddon</u>.

707. -----. <u>Why Don't the Rabbis Believe in Jesus</u>.

708. Ceperley, Gordon. <u>Would God It Were Morning</u>. n.d. 14pp.

709. <u>Hebrew Is Written from Right to Left, but the Friends of Israel...</u> N.d. 5pp.

710. <u>How Would You Recognize the Messiah?</u> 1978. 5pp.

711. Levy, David M. <u>How Can a Jewish Person Find Peace?</u> 1978. 6pp.

712. -----. <u>Intermarriage: The Jewish/Gentile Dilemma</u>. 1978. 14pp.

712a. McQuaid, Elwood. <u>Nina's New Life</u>. N.d. 7pp.

713. <u>A Mission with a Missioner</u>. 1979. 8pp.

714. Rosenthal, Marvin J. <u>Abraham Man of Faith</u>. 1976. 8pp.

715. -----. <u>Death: Hopeless Night or Glorious Sunrise?</u> 1975. 6pp.

716. -----. <u>Jehovah Sabaoth, the Lord of Hosts</u>. 1978. 7pp.

717. -----. <u>A Jew Twice Born</u>. 1976. 14pp.

718. -----. <u>The Lord's Table in the Light of the Passover</u>. 1976. 10pp.

719. -----. <u>They Made the Sepulcher Sure</u>. N.d. 8pp.

720. Rosenthal, Stanley. <u>The Kosher Heart</u>. 1975. 7pp.

721. Showers, Ronald E. <u>Behold, the Bridegroom Cometh!</u> 1975. 9pp.

722. Varner, Will. <u>Will the Real Messiah Please Stand Up</u>. 1983. 9pp.

723. Yates, Paul. <u>A People Extraordinary</u>.

724. Zutrau, Morris. <u>The Passover in the Light of the Lord's Supper</u>.

725. -----. <u>The Trinity in the Old Testament</u>.

726. -----. <u>The Virgin Birth</u>.

727. -----. <u>What's in a Name?</u>

Periodical

728. <u>Israel My Glory</u>, Box 908, Bellmawr, NJ 08031.

J. Hebrew Christians of Bridgeport, Inc.

     The Hebrews Christians of Bridgeport, Con-
necticut is a ministry headed by Isadore
Margolis. Formed in Connectitcut, it has more
recently moved its operation to Florida. It has
produced numerous tracts, many of which are
printed without publication information so they
can be used by other groups who will rubber-stamp
their own address at the end of the text. Its
most substantive publication is the _Jewish Messianic Handbook_ (originally the _Hebrew Christian
Manual_) printed as a mailer. Most of its publications are brief tracts. It has reprinted a number
of brief, select portions of Old Testament scripture without additional commentary as broadsides
(not listed below). Finally, it has also picked
up tracts from other groups and reprinted them.

729. Brickner, Albert S. _A Question of
Allegiance._ Stratford, CT: Hebrew Christians of
Bridgeport, n.d. One-page broadside.

730. _A Calendar of Jewish Persecution_. Merritt
Island, FL: n.p., n.d. One-page broadside.

731. _4 Things God Wants the Jew to Know_. Merritt
Island, FL: Hebrew Christins of Bpt., n.d. 7pp.

732. Frydland, Rachmiel. _Here Are the Facts_. Merritt Island, FL: Hebrew Christins of Bpt., n.d.
3pp.

733. -----. _The Tragedy of Mistaken Identity_.
Merritt Island, FL: n.p., n.d. 7pp.

734. _Have You Heard?_ Merritt Island, FL: Hebrew
Christians of Bpt., n.d. 4pp.

735. _The Indestructible Jew_. Merritt Island, FL:
Hebrew Christians of Bpt., n.d. 3pp.

736. Ironside, H. A. _A Search for Atoning Blood_.
Merritt Island, FL: Hebrew Christians of Bpt.,
n.d. 3pp.

737. Kelly, Howard A. _A Lovely Jewess Writes a Letter_. Merritt Island, FL: Hebrew Christians of Bpt., n.d. 4pp.

738. Margolis, Isadore. _Hebrew Christian Manual_. Stratford, CT: Hebrew Christians of Bridgeport, n.d. 13pp. Rept. as _Jewish Messianic Handbook_. Merritt Island, FL: Hebrew Christians of Bpt., Inc., n.d. 28pp.

739. -----. _The Jew and the Church_. Merritt Island, FL: Hebrew Christians of Bridgeport, n.d. 5pp.

740. _Messiah ben David_. Merritt Island, FL: n.p., n.d. 4pp.

741. _The Prophet Like Unto Moses_. Merritt Island, FL: Hebrew Christians of Bridgeport, n.d. 5pp.

742. Smith, Oswald J. _5 Solemn Facts_. Merritt Island, FL: Hebrew Christians of Bpt., n.d. 4pp.

743. Wertheimer, Max. _How a Rabbi Found Peace_. Merritt Island, FL: n.p., n.d. 8pp.

744. Wolf, Martin. _I Found Peace_. Merritt Island, FL: Hebrew Christians of Bpt., n.d. 7pp.

745. Wreschner, Lilly. _My Search for Truth_. Merritt Island, FL: Hebrew Christians of Bpt., n.d. 5pp.

K. Hebrew-Christian Publication Society

Founded in the 1890s as the Brooklyn Christian Mission to the Jews and continuing into the decade after World War I, the Hebrew-Christian Publication Society printed numerous pamphlets written by its founder-director Benjamin A. M. Shapiro. The Society circulated one book, _The Shepherd of Israel_, a novel written in Hebrew by Abraham Mapu and translated by Shapiro. It dealt with the times of Isaiah. The Society was head-quartered in New York City. For many years it published a periodical, <u>The People, the Land and the Book</u>.

746. Mapu, Abraham, <u>The Shepherd of Israel</u>. Trans. by Benjamin A. M. Shapiro. New York: B. A. M. Shapiro, 1923. 400pp.

Pamphlets
(All items authored by B. A. M. Shapiro and published by the Hebrew-Christian Publication Society in New York and undated except as noted.)

747. <u>The Christian Church and Her Jewish Neighbor</u>.

748. <u>Christian Obligations to the Jews</u>.

749. <u>The Faith of Noah</u>.

750. <u>The Genealogy of Jesus Christ</u>.

751. <u>Gethsemane in Our Lives</u>.

752. <u>The Higher Critics' Hebrew</u>.

753. <u>How the Righteousness of Christ Becomes Ours</u>.

754. <u>Jesus and His Kinsmen</u>.

755. <u>Jesus Christ a Historical Character, as Proved by the Talmud</u>.

756. <u>The Jew and the Old Testament</u>.

757. <u>The Jewish Golden Future</u>.

758. <u>Love Begets Love</u>.

759. <u>The Meaning of the Word Almoh</u>.

760. <u>The Messiah According to the Old and New Testaments</u>. 1923. 73pp. Hebrew edition. 131pp.

761. <u>The Mission of Israel</u>.

762. <u>Moses and Balaam--A Study in Contrasts</u>.

763. <u>Must Christians Keep the Jewish Sabbath?</u>
22pp.

764. <u>Our Peoples' Sin--Its Remedy</u>.

765. <u>Sacrifices, Their Origin and Significance</u>.

766. <u>Saul, The Pharisee, and Paul, the Christian</u>.
20pp.

767. <u>The Similarity Between the New Testament and the Talmud</u>.

768. <u>Some Objections to Jewish Evangelization Critically Considered</u>.

769. <u>The Sure Word of Prophecy</u>. 32pp.

770. <u>Sunday School Teaching and the Jewish People</u>.

771. <u>What Ails My People?</u>

772. <u>What the Rabbis Have to Say on the 53rd of Isaiah</u>.

773. <u>Without Him We Can DO Nothing</u>.

774. <u>Zionism--the Hope of the Jew</u>.

L. Hebrew Evangelism Society

Arthur U. Michaelson was one of the most controversial and flamboyant of the Jewish missionaries. His Los Angeles work was carried on independently of other Jewish missionary efforts, though he received much support from Mennonites. It continues today from its Los Angeles headquarters.

775. Birnbaum, Solomon. <u>The Orphan of the Polish Ghetto</u>. Los Angeles: Jewish Hope Publishing

House, n.d. 7pp.

776. Bonk, Albert D. _Israel Today_. Los Angeles:
Hebrew Evangelism Society, (1953). 18pp.

777. Michelson, Arthur Uriah. _Jesus before the
Bar_. Los Angeles: Jewish Hope Publishing Co.,
1938. 72pp.

778. -----. _From Judaism and Law to Christ and
Grace_. Los Angeles: Jewish Hope Publishing House,
1934. 129pp. Rev. ed. 1940. 144pp.

779. -----. _The Jewish Passover and the Lord's
Supper_. Los Angeles: Jewish Hope Publishing
House, n.d. 39pp. Rev. ed.: 64pp.

780. -----. _The Jews and Palestine in the Light
of Prophecy_. Los Angeles: Jewish Hope Publishing
House, 1934. 84pp. Rev. ed. 1939. 96pp. Rev. ed.
1946. 80pp.

781. -----. _Out of Darkness into Light_. Los
Angeles: Jewish Hope Publishing House, n.d. (1955
?). 127pp.

782. _A Modern Miracle Among an Ancient People_.

Periodical

783. _The Jewish Hope_.

M. International Board of Jewish Missions

In 1921, the Home Missions Board of the
Southern Baptist Church organized a Jewish
department and chose Jacob Gartenhaus as its
director. An Austrian who had been baptized in
1916 at Leopold Cohn's mission in Brooklyn, Gartenhaus attended Moody Bible Institute and the
Southern Baptist Seminary in Louisville,
Kentucky. In 1949, the Southern Baptist Church,
along with most Protestant denominations,
abolished the Jewish department. Although mis-

sions to the Jews brought the gospel to a significant number of Jews, missionary dollars could be invested in more fertile fields. In addition, any ecumenical spirit was sweeping the Christian church; for example, Baptists who could extend fellowship to Methodists and Presbyterians discovered that they could do the same to Jews. Further, many people believed that Christ's coming was imminent, and evangelism was no longer necessary.

Jacob Gartenhaus continued to solicit help from churches of various fundamental denominations, to publish <u>The Everlasting Nation</u>, and to organize small cells called "Friends of Israel." His mission prospers today in his Messianic Center in Chattanooga, Tennessee which contains a museum of Old Testament, Israeli, and miscellaneous Jewish material. The International Board of Jewish Missions supports 70 missionaries, 19 of whom work overseas in Germany, Spain, Argentina, France, England, Greece, Belgium, Venezuela, Uruguay, Brazil, Canada, and Sweden. Since the death of Dr. Gartenhaus, the board is directed by his wife, Lillian Gartenhaus, and is headquartered in Chattanooga, Tennessee.

784. Gartenhaus, Jacob. <u>Can Christians Become Jews?</u> Atlanta, GA: Cross Roads Books, 1979. 91 pp.

785. -----. <u>Christ-Killers/Past and Present</u>. Chattanooga, TN: Hebrew Christian Press, 1975. 122pp.

786. -----. <u>Famous Hebrew Christians</u>. Grand Rapids, MI: Baker Book House, 1979. 206 pp.

786a. -----. <u>How to Win the Jews</u>. Atlanta, GA: Baptist Home Mission Board, n.d. 19 pp.

787. -----. <u>The Influence of the Jews Upon Civilization</u>. Grand Rapids, MI: Zondervan Publishing House, 1943. 82 pp.

788. Number not used.

789. -----. <u>The Jew and Jesus</u>. Nashville, TN:
Sunday School Board of the Southern Baptist
Convention, 1934. 28pp.

790. -----. <u>The Jew and Jesus Christ</u>. Covington,
KY: Kentucky Bible Depot, 1934. 47 pp.

791. -----. <u>The Jewish Passover</u>. Nashville, TN:
The Author, 1944. 32pp.

792. -----. <u>An Open Letter to the Jewish People
of the South</u>. Atlanta, GA: Baptist Home Mission
Board, n.d.   16 pp.

793. -----. <u>The Rebirth of a Nation: Zionism in
History and Prophecy</u>. Nashville, TN: Broadman
Press, 1936. 131pp.

794. -----. <u>The Ten Lost Tribes</u>. Atlanta, GA:
Home Mission Board, Southern Baptist Convention,
1983. 61 pp.

795. -----. <u>Traitor? A Jew, a Book, a Miracle: An
Autobiography</u>. Nashville, TN: Nelson, 1980.
284pp.

796. -----. <u>Who Are We? What Do We Believe? What
Do We Want?</u> Atlanta, GA: Publicity Department,
Baptist Home Mission Board, n.d. 16pp.

797. -----. <u>Who Is He?</u> Atlanta, GA: Baptist
Home Mission Board, n.d.   30 pp.

798. -----. <u>Winning Jews to Christ</u>. 3rd ed.
Murfreesboro, TN: Sword of the Lord Publishers,
1976.   182 pp. Rev. ed. as: <u>Unto His Own</u>.
Atlanta,GA: International Board of Jewish
Missions, 1965.

Tracts

799. <u>Famine...Not of Bread but of Hearing the
Word.</u>" Atlanta, GA: International Board of Jewish
Missions, n.d. 7pp.

800. <u>Give Ye Them to Eat</u>. Atlanta, GA: International Board of Jewish Missions, n.d. 5pp.

801. Gartenhaus, Jacob. <u>The Jews Contribution to the South</u>. Nashville, TN: Sunday School Board of the Southern Baptist Convention, n.d. 16 pp.

802. -----. <u>An Urgent Call on Behalf of the Jews of the South</u>. Atlanta, GA: Baptist Home Mission Board, n.d. 12 pp.

803. -----. <u>10 Thousand Miles to Win a Soul</u>. Atlanta, GA: International Board of Jewish Missions, n.d. 7pp.

804. -----. <u>What of the Jews?</u> Atlanta, GA: Home Mission Board, Southern Baptist Convention, 1948.

Article

805. Gartenhaus, Jacob. "How to Approach the Jew with the Gospel." <u>Christianity Today</u> (December 9, 1966) 253-55.

Periodical

806. <u>The Everlasting Nation</u>. Box 1256, Atlanta, GA 30301

N. International Ministries to Israel (formerly:
American Association for Jewish Evangelism)

       Founded in 1945 by Hyman Appelman, the
American Association for Jewish Evangelism is
closely related to the Moody Bible Institute. The
Rev. Harry A. Ironside, pastor of Moody Memorial
Church of Chicago, helped in the establishment of
the society and served on its board of directors
for 5 years. The association currently supports
one missionary in Israel and two in Mexico. Its
outreach is conducted through radio, film production and distribution. Its budget is over
$62,000.00 per year, and it is headquartered in
Chicago, IL.

807. Appelman, Hyman Jedidiah. _Appelman's Sermon
Outlines and Illustrations_. Grand Rapids, MI: Zondervan Publishing House, 1944. 129pp.

808. -----. _The Battle of Armegeddon_. Grand
Rapids, MI: Zondervan Publishing House, 1954.
62pp.

809. -----. _The Call to Conversion_. New York:
Fleming H. Revell, 1942. 128pp.

810. -----. _Christ for America_. New York: Fleming
H. Revell, 1943.

811. Number not used.

812. -----. _Christ Is Our Strength_. New York:
Fleming H. Revell, 1948. 120pp.

813. -----. _Come Unto Me_. Grand Rapids, MI: Zondervan Publishing House, 1945. 122pp.

814. -----. _Effective Outlines and Illustrations_.
Grand Rapids, MI: Zondervan Publishing House,
1949. 122pp.

815. -----. _The Gospel of Salvation_. New York:
Fleming H. Revell, 1941. 155pp.

816. -----. _Pointed Sermon Outlines and
Illustrations_. Grand Rapids, MI: Zondervan Pub-

lishing House, 1953. 118pp.

817. -----. <u>The Saviour's Invitation</u>. Grand Rapids, MI: Zondervan Publishing House, 1944. 171pp.

818. -----. <u>Will the Circle Be Unbroken?</u> Grand Rapids, MI: Zondervan Publishing House, 1944. 171pp.

819. -----. <u>Ye Must Be Born Again</u>. Grand Rapids, MI: Zondervan Publishing House, 1939. 142pp.

820. Bradbury, John W., ed. <u>Hastening the Day of God</u>. Wheaton, IL:Van Kampen Press, 1953. 262pp.

821. -----. <u>Israel's Restoration</u>. New York: The Iversen-Ford Associates, [1954?]. 191pp.

822. Reese, Ed. <u>The Life and Ministry of Hyman Appelman</u>. Glenwood, Il: Fundamental Publishers, 1975. 15pp.

823. Number not used.

824. Stover, Gerald L., ed. <u>The Plight of the Jew</u>. New York: Loizeaux Brothers, Inc., Bible Truth Depot, n.d. 190pp.

Tracts and Pamphlets
(All published in Chicago by the American Association for Jewish Evangelism and undated, unless otherwise noted.)

825. Appelman, Hyman J. <u>Antichrist and the Jew</u>. Grand Rapids, MI: Zondervan Publishing House, 1950. 25pp.

826. -----. <u>The Atomic Bomb and the End of the World</u>. Grand Rapids, MI: Zondervan Publishing House, 1954. 28pp.

827. -----. <u>God's Answer to Man's Sin</u>. Grand Rapids, MI: Zondervan Publishing House, 1940. 5pp.

828. -----. <u>Hell. What Is It</u>. Grand Rapids, MI:

Zondervan Publishing House, 1947. 25pp.

829. -----. <u>The Jew in History and Destiny</u>. Grand Rapids, MI: Zondervan Publishing House, 1947. 27pp.

830. Culbertson, William. <u>To the Jew First</u>. 19pp.

831. Gade, Ralph. <u>Converted or Completed</u>. 5pp.

832. -----. <u>The Geneology of Messiah</u>. 14pp.

833. -----. <u>What Is a Christian?</u> 7pp.

834. -----. <u>What Is Messianic Judaism?</u> 3pp.

835. Gerber, Marvin. <u>I Am a Hebrew Christian</u>. 11pp.

836. Hoyt, Herman. <u>The Place of the United States in the Prophecy of the End Time</u>. 13pp.

837. <u>How Your Church Can Support Jewish Missions...</u> 5pp.

838. <u>The Indestructible Jew</u>. 12pp.

839. Kac, Arthur W. <u>Can a Jew Become a Follower of Jesus Christ and Remain a Jew?</u> 24pp.

840. Machlin, A. B. <u>Israel... A People of Tragedy and Promise</u>. 10pp.

841. <u>The Ministry of the American Association for Jewish Evangelism</u>. 6pp. (Periodically revised and updated)

842. <u>The Names of Jesus</u>. 7pp.

843. <u>Principle of Approach to Jewish People</u>. 13pp.

844. G. L. S. <u>"How Shall They Believe."</u> 3pp.

845. -----. <u>What About Messiah?</u> 20pp.

846. -----. <u>Who Hath Believed Our Report?</u> 12pp.

847. -----. <u>Why Missions to the Jews?</u> 8pp.

848. Wallace, W. R. _If God Didn't Write the Bible, Who Did?_ 18pp.

849. _A Well-balanced Missionary Program._ 3pp.

850. Wertheimer, Max. _How a Rabbi Found Peace._ 11pp.

851. Wilson, Walter Lewis. _A Great God for a Great People in a Great Land._ 7pp.

Periodical

852. _Salvation._ 5860 N. Lincoln Avenue, Chicago, IL 60645.

O. Israel's Evangelistic Missions, Inc.

     This group was founded in 1960 by Ben David
Lew, who was born in Poland in 1922. His plans
to become an orthodox rabbi were interrupted when
the Nazis seized his family and sent him to
Buchenwald. After his rescue by American forces,
he worked with the United Nations Refugee Relief
Association which assisted the millions of home-
less and destitute victims of the war. He helped
many Jews go to Palestine in 1945 and after his
marriage to Esther Chenkin, he emigrated to the
U.S. He arrived in New York in 1947 and soon
found himself attracted to a Jewish Christian
center where he began to study the New Testament.
Both he and his wife were baptized in 1950 and
became active in a fundamentalist Baptist church.
Deciding to become a missionary to the Jews, Lew
enrolled in the Northeastern Bible Institute in
Essex Falls, NJ and graduated in the spring of
1959.

     Since New York already had many missions to
the Jews, Lew headed for the west coast, but was
convinced to settle in Detroit. He was intro-
duced to a number of fundamentalist pastors who
promised their support, and in 1960 he began
Israel's Evangelistic Missions. The mission got
going when the owner of station WEXL, a Christian
radio station in Detroit, invited him to
broadcast. His programs are now heard in such
diverse cities as Atlanta; Boca Raton, Florida;
Tulsa, Oklahoma; and Detroit. The mission issues
a quarterly magazine, <u>The Hope of Israel</u>, and Lew
travels widely to conduct evangelistic meetings.
The organization has its headquarters in Oak
Park, Michigan.

853. Birnbaum, Solomon. <u>An Old Problem Solved</u>.
Oak Park, MI: Ben David Lew, n.d. 7pp.

854. ------. <u>Ten Gentiles and One Jews</u>. Oak Park,
MI: Israel's Evangelistic Missions, Inc., n.d.
5pp.

855. Hewitt, Phyllis. <u>Testimony of a Full Bloodied Jewess</u>. Oak Park, MI: Israel's Evangelistic Missions, Inc., n.d. 7pp.

856. Kent, Agnes S. <u>Ben and Rachel</u>. Oak Park, MI: Israel's Evangelistic Missions, Inc., n.d. 6pp.

857. Lew, Ben David. <u>Debtors to the Jews</u>. Oak Park, MI: The Author, n.d. 5pp.

858. ------. <u>From Hitler's Hell to God's Peace</u>. Oak Park, MI: Israel's Evangelistic Mission, n.d. 200pp.

859. ------. <u>God's Controversy with Israel</u>. Oak Park, MI: Israel's Evangelistic Missions, Inc., n.d. 5pp.

860. ------. <u>"Jacob Become Israel."</u> Oak Park, MI: Israel's Evangelistic Missions, Inc., n.d. 5pp.

861. ------. <u>Must Messiah Be Virgin-Born?</u> Oak Park, MI: Israel's Evangelistic Mission, n.d. 5pp.

862. ------. <u>A Soul in Hell</u>. Oak Park, MI: Israel's Evangelistic Missions, Inc., n.d. 5pp.

863. ------. <u>Thoughts on Hanukkah--The Feast of Dedication</u>. Oak Park, MI: By the author, n.d. 6pp.

864. Lew, Esther. <u>Testimony of a Hebrew Christian</u>. Oak Park, MI: Israel's Evangelsitic Missions, n.d. 5pp.

865. Miekowski, Arthur. <u>A Jewish Boy Found the Messiah</u>. Oak Park, MI: Israel's Evangelistic Missions, Inc., n.d. 4pp.

866. Moschi, Leah. <u>Hebrew Christian Testimony</u>. Oak Park, MI: Israel's Evangelistic Missions, Inc., n.d. 6pp.

Periodical

867. <u>The Hope of Israel</u>, Box 37034, Oak Park, MI
48237

P. Jewish Voice Broadcasts

     Founded in December of 1966, the Jewish
Voice Broadcasts reaches a vast audience through
radio and television broadcasts in over 30 states
and 6 countries. Its founder, Louis Kaplan, had
been a Christian evangelist for 20 years when he
heard the call to leave the evangelistic field to
start a radio broadcast to the Jewish people.
From its beginning in Phoenix, his work has expanded to some 70 stations across the nation.
His goal is to reach every Jew in the world.
Like many American Jewish Christian leaders,
Kaplan has conducted evangelistic trips to Israel
and he supports the State of Israel. Kaplan
directs the Phoenix Messianic Congregation and
publishes a monthly entitled, <u>Jewish Voice
Prophetic Magazine</u>. The headquarters are in
Phoenix, Arizona.

868. Cooper, Clay. Hippieism Unmasked in Spokane
Pulpit. Phoenix: Jewish Voice Broadcast, 1970.
8pp.

869. <u>Jewish Doctor Finds Christ</u>. Phoenix: Jewish
Voice Broadcast, n.d. 7pp.

870. Kaplan, Lewis. <u>Oh Judah, What Shall I Do
Unto Thee</u>.

871. -----. <u>The Voice of the Messsianic Jews</u>.

872. Schneider, Abraham. <u>When a Jew Finds Jesus
Christ</u>. Phoenix: Jewish Voice Broadcast, n.d.
6pp.

Periodical

873. <u>Jewish Voice Prophetic Magazine</u>, Phoenix, AZ.

Q. The Lederer Foundation

     Under the leadership of Henry Einspruch (1893-1977), a Jew who accepted Jesus and was ordained by the Lutheran Church, the Lederer Foundation was founded in 1920. Supported by Louis and Harriet Lederer, the foundation has published a number of important books, including Dr. Einspruch's Yiddish translation of the New Testament. Many of its publications are given free to Jewish inquirers and to workers in the field. Its headquarters are in Baltimore, Maryland.

874. Einspruch, Henry. <u>The Good News According to Matthew</u>. 84 pp. Rept.: Baltimore, MD: The Mediator, 1939. 120pp. Rept.: Baltimore: The Lewis and Harriet Lederer Foundation, 1964. 83pp.

875. -----. <u>The Gospel of Matthew</u> (In Yiddish). 96pp.

876. -----. <u>Jewish Confessors of the Faith</u>. Brooklyn, NY: American Borad of Missions to the Jews, 1925. 35pp.

877. -----,ed. <u>When Jews Face Christ</u>. Baltimore, MD: The Mediator, 1932.

878. -----. <u>The Yiddish New Testament</u>. 1941. 566pp.

879. Einspruch, Henry and Marie. <u>Raisins and Almonds</u>. Baltimore: The Lewis and Harriett Lederer Foundation, 1967. 87pp.

880. -----. <u>Would I? Would you?</u> Baltimore: The Lewis and Harriett Lederer Foundation, 1970.

93pp.

881. -----.   The Ox...The Ass...The Oyster...
Baltimore: The Lewis and Harriett Lederer
Foundation, 1975. 90pp.

882. Einspruch, M. G. _A Way in the Wilderness_.
100pp.

883. _The Man with the Book_. Baltimore: The
Lederer Foundation, 1970. 19pp.

884. _What Is the Lederer Foundation?_ Baltimore:
Lederer Foundation, n.d. 7pp.

Periodical

885. _The Mediator_. (Baltimore), 1928-1963.

R. Messengers of the New Covenant, Inc.

     Organized in 1941, the Messengers of the New
Covenant is a fellowship of Hebrew-Christians who
preach the gospel of Jesus in northern and
central New Jersey. Its general director is Mottel Baleston. The congregation, which is headquartered in Montclair, New Jersey, worships on
Friday nights.

886. Frydland, Rachmiel. _I Escaped from the
Nazis_. Newark, NJ: Messengers of the New
Covenant, n.d. 7pp.

887. -----. _Why I Believe_. Newark, NJ. Messengers
of the New Covenant, n.d. 8 pp.

888. _Jesus Christ, Superstar?_ Newark, NJ: Messengers of the New Covenant, n.d. 7pp.

S. Million Testaments Campaigns, Inc.

     Founded in 1923 to publish the New Testament
in various languages, this organization's evangelistic efforts are largely focused on Jews.
Their New American Standard New Testament is
called the Prophecy Edition because it includes
the Old Testament prophecies concerning the coming of the Messiah. It is free to missionaries
on request, and is widely used by many Jewish
Christian evangelistic groups. The group has a
small budget of approximately 25,000 dollars per
year and is headquartered in Philadelphia.

(All titles published in Philadelphia by Million
Testaments Campaigns)

889. Davis, George T.B. Adventures in Soul
Winning. 1942. 95pp.

890. -----. Bible Prophecies Fulfilled Today.
1955. 106pp.

891. -----. Caleb Maccabee. 1934. 246pp.

892. -----. Fulfilled Prophecies that Prove the
Bible. 1931. 123 pp.

892a.-----.   Israel Returns Home According to
Prophecy. 1950. 114pp.

893. -----. Jewels for Messiah's Crown. 1939. 95
pp.

894. -----. Rebuilding Palestine According to
Prophecy. 1935. 128pp.

895. -----. Seeing Prophecy Fulfilled in
Palestine. 1937. 134pp.

896. -----. Sowing God's Word in Israel Today.
1953. 137pp.

897. -----. When the Fire Fell. 1945. 107pp.

898. -----, and Rose F. Davis.   God's Guiding

<u>Hand</u>. 1962. 254pp.

899. Finestone, Olive Deane. <u>The Romantic Career of a Twice-Born Jewess</u>. 1941. 96pp.

900. <u>A Jew, a Book, and a Miracle</u>. N.d. 32pp.

901. Levy, Asher. <u>Rabbi Sher Levy Speaks to This Generation</u>. N.d. 22pp.

902. <u>New American Standard New Testament, Old Testament Prophecy Edition</u>. 1960. 64pp.

903. <u>Out of Darkness Into Light</u>. n.d. 23pp.

Articles

904. Davis, George T. B. "The Miracle of the Jews Regathering." <u>The Sunday School Times</u> (October 1, 1955) 771-72.

905. -----. A Divine Promise that Changed History." <u>The Sunday School Times</u> 99, 11 (March 16, 1957) 205-06, 222.

T. Moody Bible Institute

Founded in 1899 by Dwight L. Moody, the Moody Bible Institute has become the training ground for many Jewish Christian evangelists. The Institute has a Jewish Department that has won the respect of those who oppose evangelism to the Jews. Its students are drawn from many churches and ministries and it works with the variety of existing Jewish Christian groups more or less impartially. Many of its graduates go to Gentile churches while more recently, some are serving messianic congregations. The institute, whose library is one of the principal sources of Jewish Christian material in America, is located in Chicago, Illinois. Louis Goldberg is Professor of Theology and Jewish Studies at Moody.

906. Franzen, Jan. "Lure of the Holy Land."
<u>Christian Life</u> 41, 4 (August 1979) 20-22, 55-56.

907. Goldberg, Louis. "How to Bridge the Jewish-
Christian Gap." <u>Christian Life</u> 41, 4 (August
1979) 23, 40-45.

908. -----. <u>Our Jewish Friends</u>. Chicago: Moody
Press, 1977. 188pp. Rept.: Neptune, NJ: Loizeaux
Brothers, 1983. 188pp.

909. -----. <u>Turbulence Over the Middle East</u>.

910. Raney, Dave. "A Converted Russian Jew at
MBI." <u>Moody Monthly</u> 78, 4 (December 1977) 104-6.

U. Morris Cerullo World Evangelism, Inc.

Morris Cerullo, who had an Italian father
and a Jewish mother, spent his early childhood in
a strict Jewish orthodox orphanage. At the age
of 14 he accepted Jesus as the Messiah and at 15
he felt called to become an evangelist. During
the 1950s he was briefly associated with William
Branham and Oral Roberts. In the years since, he
has preached to audiences in over 40 countries,
including: Korea, India, Brazil, and the United
States. The ministry was organized in 1961 as
Morris Cerullo World Evangelism; its headquarters
are in San Diego, California.

Although most of his listeners are gentiles,
he has the vision of reaching "every Jew in the
world at least once before Jesus comes again."
To assist in that goal, he has produced a film,
"Masada," which has been shown on television and
in hundreds of churches and public halls
throughout the world. In the early 1970s he published Bible study course to Jews, <u>Besorat
Shalom</u>, published as a series of undated 4-page
lessons, and has claimed remarkable success for
some of his books and booklets. According to his
organization, copies of <u>Two Men From Eden</u> were

shipped to 3,200,000 Jewish homes in North America, at a cost of over $700,000. Further, as a result of reading this book, 7,000 people were moved to receive Jesus.

(All published by World Evangelism in San Diego, except as noted)

911. Balliet, Emil A. and Morris Cerullo. _Who Will Win the War in the Middle East?_ 1970. 60pp.

912. Cerullo, Morris. _The Back Side of Satan_. Carol Stream, IL: Creation House, 1973. 224pp.

913. -----. _Breakthrough in Prophecy_. 1971. 30pp.

914. -----. _Confess the Promise Out_. 1977. 30pp.

915. -----. _Day Stars_. 1981. 70pp.

916. -----. _Day Stars II_. 1982. 70pp.

917. -----. _Financial Power Pact_. 1982. 32pp.

918. -----. _From Judaism to Christianity_. 1962. 86pp.

919. -----. _God Has a Plan for Your Life...Your New Life!_ 1986. 41pp.

920. -----. _God is Stirring a Miracle for You!_ 1985. 16pp.

921. -----. _God's Answers to Your Questions_. 1983. 54pp.

922. -----. _God's Healing River_. 1964. 6pp.

923. -----. _God's Master Plan of the Ages_. 1971. 31pp.

924. -----. _God's Will For Your Life_. 1984. 103pp.

925. -----. _A Guide to Total Health and Prosperity_. 1977. 157pp.

926. -----. _How to Have the Power of God_. 1977. 27pp.

927. -----. _How to Take the Limit Off of God_. 1978. 82pp.

928. -----. _How to Win the Battle of Life_. 1973. 32pp.

929. -----. _How You Can Defeat Satan_. 1980. 279pp.

930. -----. _"I Care" Prayer Ministry_. 1978. 63pp.

931. -----. _Israel, Land of Prophecy_.

932. -----. _Jesus Christ Our Great High Priest_.

933. -----. _The Key to Spiritual Success_. 1965. 32pp.

934. -----. _Making Possible Your Impossibilities_. 1972. 32pp.

935. -----. _The Miracle Book_. 1984. 169pp.

936. -----. _Miracles Happen When Someone Cares_. 1975. 110pp.

937. -----. _My Life Story_. 1965. 86pp.

938. -----. _The New Anointing_. 1975. 147pp.

939. -----. _The New Anointing, the Healing of the Home_. 1975. 19pp.

940. -----. _The New Anointing is Here_. 1972. 44pp.

941. -----. _The Omega Project_. 1981. 82pp.

942. -----. _One Demon Spirit_. 1985. 77pp.

943. -----. _Proof Producers_. 1972. 90pp.

944. -----. _Revelation Healing Power_. 1979. 104pp.

945. -----. _The Seven Greatest Signs of the Second Coming of Jesus Christ_. 1985. 36pp.

946. -----. _Seven Steps to Victory for Body, Soul, Spirit_. 1955. 32pp.

947. -----. _The Shaking Has Started...1980_. 99pp.

948. -----. _Spiritual Breakthrough in Prophecy_. 1971. 29pp.

949. -----. _Taking God's Power_. 1978. 26pp.

950. -----. _Two Men From Eden_. 1977. 150pp.

951. -----. _The Unholy Unity_. 1986. 40pp.

952. -----. _Upon Wings as an Eagle_. 1975. 29pp.

953. -----. _Victory Miracle Living--It's Harvest Time_. 1982. 102pp.

954. -----. _What Does This Mean?_

955. -----. _Why Do the Righteous Suffer?_ 1978. 130pp.

956. -----. _Wind Over the Twentieth Century_. 1973. 67pp.

957. -----. _You Can Know How to Defeat Satan_. 1980. 278pp.

958. Cerullo, Theresa. _Through Moments of Change_.

959. Hull, William. _Israel, Key to Prophecy_. Grand Rapids: Zondervan Publishing House, n.d. 104pp.

960. -----. _Will the Jews Rebuild the Temple?_ N.d. 9pp.

Articles

961. Roddy, Lee. "Morris Cerullo Crusade: A New Anointing." _Christianity Today_ (February 18,

1972), 52-53.

Periodicals

962. <u>Deeper Life</u>. San Diego, 1961-1982.

963. <u>It's Happening Now</u>. Morris Cerullo World Evangelism, Inc., Box 700, San Diego, CA 92138

964. <u>Victory</u>. Morris Cerullo World Evangelism, Inc., Box 700, San Diego, CA 92138

V. The New Covenent Mission

The New Covenant Mission of Pittsburgh, Pennsylvania was founded by Maurice Reuben and has carried on a ministry in Western Pennsylvania for many years. For a short time, Max Wertheimer pastored the congregation and was the chief evangelist.

965. Wertheimer, Max. <u>Why I Left Christian Science</u>. Ada, OH: The Author, 1916. 60pp.

966. -----. <u>From Rabbinism to Christ</u>. Ada, OH: Wertheimer Publications, 1934. 91pp.

967. -----. <u>Satan</u>. Ada, OH: Wertheimer Publications, 1934. 61pp.

968. -----. <u>The Time of Jacob's Trouble</u>. New York: Angel Memorial House, New York Gospel Mission to the Jews, n.d. 10pp.

W. Pacific Garden Mission

Founded in 1877 by George and Sarah Clarke, the Pacific Garden Mission works on Chicago's southside skid row in a varied and successful ministry. In 1950, it began to produce the radio program, "Unshackled," which broadcast on 230 stations in the U.S. and in 12 foreign countries on 6 continents. An estimated 10 million people hear "Unshackled" each week. The mission has a separate Jewish department which produces tracts to evangelize Jews: these are used by the large staff of the Pacific Garden Mission and other Jewish Christian missions in the Chicago area. Its headquarters are near the Chicago Loop where a mission for the unfortunate and a center for servicemen are maintained.

969. Adair, James R. _The Old Lighthouse_. Chicago, IL: The Pacific Garden Mission. 1966. 157pp.

970. Jacobson, Hezekiah. _Messiah's Coming Prophesied in the Tenach!_ Chicago, IL: Pacific Garden Mission, n.d. 3pp.

X. Rock of Israel, Inc.

The Rock of Israel started in 1969 while Hyman and Dorothy Specter were serving as missionaries in Senegal, French West Africa. Their ministry consists of radio and television broadcasts and the distribution of vast quantities of literature. Hyman Specter was born in 1918 in Los Angeles of Orthodox Jewish parents who raised him in the Jewish religion. In 1938, his mother and sister became convinced that Jesus was the Messiah and shortly thereafter Specter became a missionary in Haiti and West Africa. He served as a dentist and preacher in a Protestant mission in Haiti for 13 years. Later he and his wife, Dorothy, worked to reach the Jewish people through the Rock of Israel Ministries. Dorothy Specter died in 1978, and in the latter part of 1979, Hyman Specter married a gentile Christian, Dori Corral, who joined the ministry and serves as co-director. Specter's sister, Ruth Specter Lascelle, is active in the ministry and has written most of the pamphlets published by the Rock of Israel. The ministry currently has branches in San Diego and in Brazil. It is headquartered in Van Nuys, California.

971. Lascelle, Ruth Specter. _That They Might Be Saved_. Seattle, WA: Bedrock Press, 1978. 44pp.

972. -----. _Who Was Responsible for the Death of Christ?_ Van Nuys, CA: Rock of Israel, n.d. 22pp.

973. -----. _One Way Passage_. Tarzana, CA: Rock of Israel, n.d. 10pp.

974. Sims, M. _Can You Answer These Questions Taken from the Tenach?_ Translated by Isaac Leeser, Van Nuys, CA: Rock of Israel, n.d. 10pp.

975. Specter, Dorothy. _Their Debtors We Are_. Tarzana, CA: Rock of Israel, 1971. 17pp.

976. -----. _A Study in Prophecy_. Van Nuys, CA: Rock of Israel, n.d. 11pp.

977. Specter, Ruth R. _The Bud and the Flower of Judaism_. Springfield, MO: Gospel Publishing House, 1955. 310pp

Tracts
(As noted, these tracts are part of a numbered series.)

978. _Are You A ...Christian?_ Van Nuys, CA: Rock of Israel, n.d. 3pp. (31)

979. _Are You a True Jew?_ Van Nuys, CA: Rock of Israel, n.d. 5 pp. (45)

980. Banks, John C. _Every Jew Stands Challenged_. Tarzana, CA: Rock of Israel, n.d. 6pp.

981. Baron, David. _The Religion of My Fathers_. Van Nuys, CA: Rock of Israel, n.d. 5pp. (20)

982. _The Christian Attitude Toward Jewish Evangelism_. Van Nuys, CA: Rock of Israel, n.d. 3pp.

983. Dallman, Ruth. <u>The Light of My Life</u>. Van Nuys, CA: Rock of Israel, n.d. 6pp. (29)

984. Feinberg, Charles L. <u>4 Things God Wants the Jew to Know</u>. Tarzana, CA: Rock of Israel, n.d. 7 pp. (36)

985. <u>Four Things That--God Wants YOU to Know</u>. Van Nuys, CA: Rock of Israel, n.d. 7pp. (30)

986. Glauberg, Joe and Rhoda Glauberg. <u>One In the Lord</u>. Van Nuys, CA: Rock of Israel, n.d. 6pp.

987. Horne, Thomas H. <u>Tree of Bible Facts</u>. Tarzana, CA: Rock of Israel, n.d. 1p. (51)

988. <u>If the Messiah Comes, How Will We Know Him?</u> Van Nuys, CA: Rock of Israel, n.d. 6pp. (5)

989. "It Is Written." Van Nuys, CA: Rock of Israel, n.d. 3pp. (27)

990. Lascelle, Ruth S. <u>Abraham Believed God's Promise--Do You?</u> Van Nuy, CA: Rock of Israel, n.d. 4pp. (46)

991. -----. <u>An Atonement for Israel</u>. Van Nuys, CA: Rock of Israel, n.d. 4pp. (38)

992. -----. <u>Brith Milah</u>. Tarzana, CA: Rock of Israel, n.d. 3pp. (6)

993. -----. <u>Christianity Is Jewish</u>. Van Nuys, CA: Rock of Israel, n.d. 5 pp. (16)

994. -----. <u>Dear Jewish Reader: God Loves You!</u> Van Nuys, CA: Rock of Israel, n.d. 4 pp.

995. -----. <u>The First and the Last</u>. Tarzana, CA: Rock of Israel, n.d. 3pp. (42)

996. -----. <u>Five Reasons for Evangelizing THE JEW</u>. Van Nuys, CA: Rock of Israel, n.d. 5pp. (26)

997. -----. <u>God Loves You</u>. Van Nuys, CA: Rock of Israel, n.d. 3pp. (430)

998. -----. <u>God Who Became Man</u>. Van Nuys, CA: Rock of Israel, n.d. 6pp. (47)

999. -----. <u>Hear! O Jew and Gentile!</u> Van Nuys, CA: Rock of Israel, n.d. 4pp. (4)

1000. -----. <u>The Holy Spirit</u>. Van Nuys, CA: Rock of Israel, n.d. 4pp. (8)

1001. -----. <u>I Have Found Him!</u> Van Nuys, CA: Rock of Israel, 1983. 5pp.

1002. -----. <u>Jews Should Know</u>. Van Nuys, CA: Rock of Israel, n.d. 6pp. (1)

1003. -----. <u>King of the Jews</u>. Van Nuys, CA: Rock of Israel, n.d. (12)

1004. -----. <u>Kosher</u>. Van Nuys, CA: Rock of Israel, n.d. 3pp. (7)

1005. -----. <u>The Lamb of Exodus</u>. Van Nuys, CA: Rock of Israel, n.d. 6pp.

1006. -----. <u>"Let My People Go."</u> Van Nuys, CA: Rock of Israel, n.d. 2pp. (24)

1007. -----. <u>The Lost Sheep of the House of Israel</u>. Van Nuys, CA: Rock of Israel, n.d. (14)

1008. -----. <u>Messiah in the Hebrew Scriptures</u>. Van Nuys, CA: Rock of Israel, n.d. 6pp. (52)

1009. -----. <u>Messiah to Be a Prophet, Priest and King!</u> Van Nuys, CA: Rock of Israel, n.d. 2pp. (25)

1010. -----. <u>Messiah to Be Like Moses</u>. Van Nuys, CA: Rock of Israel, n.d. (15)

1011. -----. <u>Moses and the Serpent</u>. Tarzana, CA: Rock of Israel, n.d. 6pp. (47)

1012. -----. <u>The Name "Jehovah."</u> Van Nuys, CA: Rock of Israel, n.d. 3pp. (48)

1013. -----. <u>Signs of Messiah's Return</u>. Van Nuys, CA: Rock of Israel, n.d. 5pp. (3)

1014. -----. _Some Original Jewish Contributions_. Tarzana, CA: Rock of Israel, n.d. 5pp. (9)

1015. -----. _A Rabbi Searches the Scriptures_. Van Nuys, CA: Rock of Israel, n.d. 5pp. (2)

1016. -----. _A Story of Passover_. Van Nuys, CA: Rock of Israel, n.d. 6pp. (23)

1017. -----. _A Supposed Imposter Becomes My Messiah_. Van Nuys, CA: Rock of Israel, n.d. 6pp.

1018. -----. _The Three Matzoth of the Passover Seder_. Van Nuys, CA: Rock of Israel, 1977. 1p. (50)

1019. -----. _Who Is a Jew?_ Van Nuys, CA; Rock of Israel, n.d. 4pp. (13)

1020. -----. _Who Is the Rock of Israel?_ Van Nuys, CA: Rock of Israel, n.d. 4pp. (37)

1021. -----. _Who Was Responsible for the Death of Christ?_ Van Nuys, CA: Rock of Israel, n.d. 22pp. (17)

1022. Le-Israel, Eduth. _Come Let Us Reason Together_. Van Nuys, CA: Rock of Israel, n.d. 4pp. (21)

1023. Madono, Teruko L. _Inner Peace_. Van Nuys, CA: Rock of Israel, n.d. (54)

1024. _The Messiah_. Van Nuys, CA: Rock of Israel, n.d. 2pp. (32)

1025. _Of Whom Did Isaiah Write?_ Van Nuys, CA: Rock of Israel, n.d. 4pp. (53)

1026. _One Way Passage_. Tarzana, CA: Rock of Israel, n.d. 10pp. (35)

1027. Proctor, O. Sturdy. _Cacoethes (A Bad Habit-Mania)_. Tarzana, CA: Rock of Israel, n.d. 3pp.

1028. _Rock of Israel, Inc_. Van Nuys, CA: Rock of Israel, n.d. 2pp.

1029. Rosenthal, Jacob. _A Jewish Testimony_. Van Nuys, CA: Rock of Israel, n.d. 5pp. (22)

1030. _Some Jews Have Said_. Van Nuys, CA: Rock of Israel, n.d. 5 pp. (19)

1031. _Something to Think About!_ Van Nuys, CA: Rock of Israel, n.d. 6pp. (44)

1032. Specter, Anne. _"I Have Found Him."_ Van Nuys, CA: Rock of Israel, n.d. 4pp. (11)

1033. Specter, Dori J. _The Man in the White Coat_. Van Nuys, CA: Rock of Israel, n.d. 5pp. (55)

1034. Specter, Dorothy Graves. The Christian Attitude Toward Jewish Evangelism. Van Nuys, CA: Rock of Israel, n.d. 3pp. (28)

1035. Specter, Hyman Israel. _A Jew Accepts His Messiah_. Van Nuys, CA: Rock of Israel, 6pp.

1036. _A Study in Prophecy_. Van Nuys, CA: Rock of Israel, n.d. 11pp. (33)

1037. _The Tabernacle of God_. Van Nuys, CA: Rock of Israel, n.d. 4pp. (40)

1038. Torrey, R. A. _Two Geneologies of Messiah_. Van Nuys, CA: Rock of Israel, n.d. 4pp. (56)

1039. _The Way of Salvation_. Van Nuys, CA: Rock of Israel, n.d. 31pp. (39).

1040. _What Readest Thou?_ Tarzana, CA: Rock of Israel, n.d. 3pp. (41)

1041. _Who Is a Jew?_ Van Nuys, CA: Rock of Israel, n.d. 4pp. (13)

1042. _Who Is This One?_ Van Nuys, CA: Rock of Israel, n.d. 28pp. (18)

Y. The Scott Mission

     Established in 1908 by the Foreign Mission
Board of the Presbyterian Church in Canada to
witness to the Jews in Toronto, the mission became independent in 1941. Called the Christian
synagogue, it was renamed in 1920 to honor the
Rev. J. MacPherson Scott, a long-time friend of
the synagogue. In 1926, Morris Zeidman who had
become a Christian through the ministry of the
Christian synagogue, became superintendent of the
Scott Institute. He held this post for the
remainder of his life and when he died in 1964,
the Rev. Alex Zeidman became the director. The
mission works not only among the Jews, but also
with the poor gentiles in the area, providing
Meals on Wheels and supporting a group home and a
receiving home for children near Kenora. The
headquarters are in Toronto.

Tracts
(All published by The Scott Mission, Toronto,
Canada. No dates.)

1043. Thomas, A.E. <u>The Seed of David</u>. 7pp.

1044. Number not used.

1045. <u>Who? When? Where? A Brief History of the
Scott Mission</u>. 1pp.

1046. Zeidman, Morris. <u>Are Christian Gentiles
Spiritual Jews?</u> 12pp.

1047. ------. <u>Emotion and Religion</u>. 10pp.

1048. ------. <u>Jewish Belief in Mediatorship Between God and Man</u>. 11pp.

1049. ------. <u>Major Hebrew Feasts</u>. 14pp.

1050. ------. <u>Passover Appeal to the Hebrews</u>. 7pp.

1051. ------. <u>The Pre-existent Christ Is God</u>.
16pp.

1052. -----. <u>Who Crucified Jesus?</u> 8pp.

Z. Zion Messianic House in Jerusalem and World-Wide Signs Following Evangelism

     The World-Wide Signs Following Evangelism ministry was founded by LeRoy M. Kopp who passed the leadership to his son, E. Paul Kopp. The ministry places a strong emphasis on healing, and its letterhead states that its crusades are "to the Jew first and also to the Gentiles." In 1939, LeRoy Kopp founded the United Fundamentalist church which presently supports Zion Messianic House in Jerusalem. However, the literature for the ministries stresses that they are non-denominational, while indicating that contributions pass through the United Fundamentalist church. The church has approximately 250 ministers and missionaries, many of whom are involved in the World-Wide Evangelism Signs Following ministries. E. Paul Kopp, his wife, Betty, and their son, Charles, have traveled throughout the world conducting evangelistic crusades and healing missions. In his book, <u>The Jews Require a Sign</u>, Paul Kopp argues that the Jews, in particular, need the evidence of a healing ministry to show that the ministry is from God. The group is headquartered in Los Angeles, California.

1053. Kopp, E. Paul. <u>Divine Healing and Devil Binding</u>. Los Angeles: World-Wide Signs Following Evangelsim, 1957. 62pp.

1054. -----. <u>The Jews Require a Sign</u>. Los Angeles: World-Wide Signs Following Evangelism, 1957. 62pp.

1055. -----. <u>The Truth About Divine Healing</u>. Los Angeles: World-Wide Signs Following Evangelism, 1957. 65pp.

AA. Miscellaneous and General Literature Related
to Jewish Missionary Efforts

     The literature listed below circulates
within the broader Jewish Christian Movement but
is either published independently of any specific
ministry or by those small ministries which publish only one or a few pieces of literature.

1056. Abrams, Julius H. _Out of the House of
Judah_. New York: Fleming H. Revell, 1923. 215pp.

1057. Adair, James R. _The Old Lighthouse_.
Chicago, IL: The Pacific Garden Mission, 1966.
157pp.

1058. _Aids to Jewish Evangelism_. Dallas: Dallas
Theological Seminary, 1959.

1059. Amber, Lee. _Chosen_. Santa Ana, CA: Vision
House Publishers, 1977. 142pp.

1060. _Arise and Shine_. Kansas City, MO: Lillenas
Publlishing Co., 1979.

1061-69. Numbers not used.

1070. Aston, Frederick A. _A Challenge to Every
Jew_. New York: n.p., 1934. 24pp.

1071. Baur, Benjamin. _How Has God Honored the
Jews?_ Rochester, NY: What the Bible Says, Inc.,
n.d. 96pp.

1072. Benedict, George. _Christ Finds a Rabbi: An
Autobiography_. Philadelphia: n.p., 1932.

1073. Benson, Carmen. _Jesus and Israel_. Watchung,
NJ: Charisma Books, 1971. 189pp.

1074. Brande, Morris. _Conscience on Trial_. New
York: Exposition Press, 1952. 147pp.

1075. Capp, M. _The Messiah Shown to Be Son of God
in the Old Testament_. New York: New York Gospel
Mission to the Jews, n.d. 31pp.

1076. Chalmers, Thomas Mitchell. _Under the Olive Tree_. New York: The Author, 1931. 224pp.

1077. Clifford, David. _The Two Jerusalems in Prophecy_. Neptune, NJ: Loizeaux Brothers, 1978. 192pp.

1078. Davidson, Joy. "The Longest Way Around." In David Wesley Soper, ed. _These Found the Way: Thirteen Converts to Protestant Christianity_. Philadelphia: Westminister Press, 1951.

1079. -----. _Smoke on the Mountain: An Interpretation of the Ten Commandments_. Philadelphia: Westminister Press, 1954.

1080. Dobschiner, Johanna Ruth. _Selected to Live_. Old Tappan, NJ: Flemming H. Revell, 1973. 190pp.

1081. Dorsett, Lyle W. _And God Came In_. New York: Macmillan Publishing Company, 1983. 167pp.

1082. Douermann, Stuart. _Music for the Messiah_. Kansas City, MO: Lilenas Publishing Co., 1975. Book I, 64pp. Book II, 76pp.

1083. Duff-Forbes, Lawrence. _Delving into Deuteronomy_. Whittier, CA: Congregation of the Messiah within Israel, 1973. 2 Vols.

1084. -----. _Looking into Leviticus_. Whittier, CA: Congregation of the Messiah within Israel, 1966. 52pp.

1085. -----. _Moments with the Mishkan_. Piedmont, CA: Albain Press, 1965. 73pp.

1086. -----. _Peril from the North_. Whittier, CA: Review Publishing Company, 1958. 90pp.

1087. Eckarat, Arthur R. _Christianity and the Children of Israel_. New York: King's Crown Press, 1948. 223pp.

1088. Eckstein, Stephen D. _From Sinai to Calvary: An Autobiography_. Kansas City, MO: The Author, 1959.

1089. Espar, Morton H. I Found Salvation Through a Hebrew Prayer Book. Oradell, NJ: American Tract Society, n.d. 5pp.

1090. Freedman, Benjamin. Facts Are Facts. New York: The Author, 1955. 62pp.

1091. Goldman, Joseph. Judaism and Its Traditions, The Conversion of a Hebrew Rabbi. Los Angeles: J. F. Rowny Press, 1919. 72pp.

1092. Guinness, Michele. Child of the Covenant. New York: Ballantine Books, 1985. 148pp.

1093. Hajos, Mary. The Eternal Covenant. Fort Washington, PA: Christian Literature Crusade, 1971. 113pp.

1094. A Hebrew Christian. Go Tell My People. New York: Vantage Press, 1958.

1095. Hendriksen, William. Israel and the Bible. Grand Rapids, MI: Baker Book House, 1968. 63pp.

1096. Henry, Carl F. H. "The Christian Witness in Israel." Christianity Today 5, 22 (July 31, 1961) 22-23.

1097. Hewitt, Phyllis Sokol. From Miry Clay to Solid Rock. Tulsa, OK: Tulsa Friends of Israel, 1968. 122pp.

1098. Hoffman, Conrad. The Jews Today, A Call to Christian Action. New York: Friendship Press, 1941.

1099. -----. What Now for the Jews? New York: Friendship Press, 1948.

1100. Hunting, Joseph H. Israel-A Modern Miracle. Murrumbeena, Australia: The David Press, 1969 2 Vols.

1101. -----. Israel My Son. Murrumbeena, Australia: The David Press, 1970. 46pp.

1102. Jacobson, Hezekiah. Messiah's Coming

Prophesied in the Tenach. Chicago, IL: Pacific
Garden Mission, n.d. 3pp.

1103. Jocz, Jakob. The Jewish People and Jesus
Christ. London: SPCK, 1949. Third ed.: Grand
Rapids, MI: Baker Book House, 1979. 448pp.

1104. -----. The Jewish People and Jesus Christ
after Auschwitz. Grand Rapids, MI: Baker Book
House, 1981. 273pp.

1105. Josephson, Elmer A. God's Key to Health and
Happiness. Wichita, KS: Bible Light Publications,
1962. 202pp.

1106. Katz, Arthur. Ben Israel. Plainfield, NJ:
Logos International, 1970. 185pp.

1107. -----. Reality, The Hope of Glory.
Plainfield, NJ; Logos International, 1977. 204pp.

1108. Ketcherside, W. Carl. Talks to Jews and
Non-Jews. Cincinnati, OH: Standard Publishing
Company, 1977. 176pp.

1109. Kreider, Roy. Judaism Meets Christ: Guiding
Principles for Christian Encounter. Scottdale,
PA: Herald Press, 1960.

1110. Kutner, John. "Peace of Mind." Full Gospel
Business Men's Voice 18, 3 (April 1970) 4- 7, 12.

1111. Lagona, James F. The Seder of Our Lord.
Buffalo, NY: The Author, 1983. 18pp.

1112. Lasky, William R. Tell It On the Mountain.
Garden City, NY: Doubleday, 1976. Rept.: New
York: Pocket Books, 1977. 257pp.

1113. Lee, Robert G. If I Were a Jew. Chicago
Moody Press, 1970. 62pp.

1114. Leverhoff, Paul. The Order of Service of
the Meal of the Holy King. Milwaukee: Morehouse,
1928.

1115. Littell, John S. Some Great Christian Jews.
Keene, NH: The Author, 1913. 64pp. (Stories of

Cross and Flag, No.2)

1116. M'Cheyne, Robert Murray. <u>Why Give the Gospel "To the Jew First"?</u> Memphis, TN: The Ohio Mesianic Testimony, n.d. 2pp.

1117. Macnaughtan, K. A., comp. <u>The Covenants and the Promises</u>. Carnegie, Australia: The David Press, 1970. 51pp.

1118. Markell, Jan. <u>Gone the Golden Dream</u>. Minneapolis, MN: Bethany Fellowship, 1979. 172pp.

1119. Meldau, Fred J. <u>Messiah in Both Testaments</u>. Denver: Christian Victory Publishing Company, 1956. 97pp.

1120. Neumann, Friedrich. <u>Escape from Terror</u>. New York: Exposition Press, 1959. 296pp.

1121. Ostrom, Henry. <u>The Jew and His Mission</u>. Chicago: The Bible Institute Corportage Ass'n, 1923. 157pp.

1122. Pearlmutter, Semha. <u>The Tents of Shem.</u> New York: Vantage Press, 1980. 150pp.

1123. Perl, Ruth June. <u>Thy People Will Be My People</u>. Minneapolis: Bethany Fellowship Publishers, 1968. 249pp.

1124. Phillips, McCandlish. <u>The Bible, the Supernatural and the Jews</u>. Minneapolis: Bethany Fellowship Publishers, 1973. 366pp.

1125. Photiou, Paul. <u>My Conversion to Christ</u>. Chicago: The Orthodox Christian Education Society, 1970. 16pp.

1126. Prinz, Hirsh. <u>The Great Mystery: or How Can Three Be One?</u> Nutley, NJ: Hebrew Christian Publications, 1970. 98pp.

1127. Rawlings, Meritel. <u>Fishers and Hunters</u>. Jerusalem: World Vistas, 1982. 271pp.

1128. Rothchild, Walter. <u>Can a Hebrew Also Be a Christian?</u> Jerusalem: The Author, n.d. 24pp.

1129. Roy, Kristina. _Only a Servant_. Minneapolis, MN: Osterhaus Publishing House, n.d. 62pp.

1130. Rudolph, George. _Sunshine Through Shadows_. Cleveland Heights, OH: The Author, n.d. 47pp.

1131. A. F. S., _Messianic Guide for Jews and Gentiles_. N.p.: n.d. 29pp.

1132. Schaeffer, Edith. _Christianity is Jewish_. Wheaton, IL: Tyndale House, 1975. 224pp.

1133. _A Search for the Atoning Blood_. Winnipeg, Canada: Hull Publishing Co., 4pp.

1134. Telchin, Stan. _Betrayed_. Grand Rapids, MI: Chosen Books, 1984. 139pp.

1135. Thieme, Robert B., Jr. _Anti-Semitism_. Houston, TX: Berachah Tapes and Publications, 1979. 152pp.

1136. _A Trumpet in Zion_. N.p.: n.d. 148pp.

1137. Warmer, Rose. _12 Months in the Concentration Camp_. Columbus, OH: Bible Literature International, n.d. 23pp.

1138. Wurmbrand, Richard. _Christ on the Jewish Road_. Glendale, CA: Diane Books, 1970. 192pp.

1139. -----. _Tortured for Christ_. Glendale, CA: Diane Books, 1969. 139pp.

1140. Yacovsky, F. Jacob. _The Missing 200 Years (God's Timetable)_. Fern Park, FL: Sar Sholem of Jerusalem, 1978. 108pp.

1141. _Why I Love the Jew_. Westchester, IL: Good News Publishers, n.d. 3pp.

BB. The Michael Esses Incident

     Many Jews who oppose Jewish missions com-
plain that Jewish-Christian converts often lie
about their background and claim credentials
which they have never possessed. On several occasions such accusations have proved correct. The
most recent case has been that of Michael Esses
who became a prominent leader among Pentecostals
during the 1970s and assumed a faculty position
at the Melodyland School of Theology in Anaheim,
California. Besides claiming to have been a
former rabbi, he accepted consecration from John
M. Stanley, an independent Orthodox bishop who
claims apostolic succession through the Syro-
Chaldean Church of the East. The service of consecration was held in Jerusalem (1149).

     The discovery of Esses' fraud was a major
component in the fall of the numerous Melodyland
ministries from their influential position in
evangelical circles, though there were several
other contributing factors. Following their
divorce, Betty Esses documented the whole story
in her autobiographical volume (1142).

1142. DeBlase, Betty Esses. _Survivor of a Tar-
nished Ministry_. Anaheim, CA: Truth Publishers,
1983. 188pp.

1143. Esses, Michael. The Father Didn't Forsake
Jesus and He Won't Forsake You. Covina, CA: The
Emissary, 1978. 29pp.

1144. -----. Jesus in Exodus. Plainfield,   NJ:
Logos International, 1977. 257pp.

1145. -----. _Jesus in Genesis_. Plainfield, NJ:
Logos International, 1974. 263pp.

1146. -----. _Michael, Michael, Why Do You Hate
Me?_ Plainfield, NJ: Logos International, 1974.
189pp.

1147. -----. _The Next Visitor to Planet Earth_.
Plainfield, NJ: Logos International, 1975. 173pp.

1148. -----. <u>The Phenomena of Obedience</u>. Plainfield, NJ: Logis International, 1974. 189pp.

1149. Medina, Dave. "Former Rabbi Named Chaldean Archbishop." <u>Logos Journal</u> 40, 6 (November-December 1972) 58.

SECTION FIVE

THE NEW MESSIANISM OF THE 1970S

A. The Jews for Jesus

     Jews for Jesus is the most successful and be-
st known of the various missions to the Jews. It
was created by Moishe Rosen, who had been a missionary for the American Board of Missions to the
Jews. Rosen was convinced that in order to minister to the hippies of the 1960s, he would have to
change the traditional approach and methods used
by the ABMJ. In 1970, Rosen started to work in
Corte Madera and San Francisco under the auspices
of the American Board. But by 1973, it was
mutually decided that Jews for Jesus should be a
separate work, and it was incorporated as the
Hineni Missions.

     The new group was different from any other
mission to the Jews in many respects. First, it
sought out, not conservative scholars, but those
who were estranged both from Judaism and society.
Second, just as Martin Rosen rediscovered his
Jewishness, and he chose to be known as Moishe
Rosen, the group reclaimed much of its Jewish culture observing traditions such as the Pesach Seder
which are not incompatible with the Christian
faith. They also sang the Kiddush, the initial
blessing over meals, and wrote their own Haggadah,
the historical narrative of how the Jews escaped
the Pharaoh.

     Two characteristics of the group have aroused
considerable opposition in certain elements of the
Jewish community. The Jews for Jesus, first of

all, insist that they are Jews and that as a result of their acceptance of Jesus as Messiah they are "completed Jews." This first affront to the Jewish community is combined with a second, the use of aggressive tactics in evangelizing their Jewish neighbors. Wherever Jews are found in great numbers, the Jews for Jesus appear with smiles and literature. They have also taken out full page advertisements in leading papers across the country, including the New York Times, which proclaim that "The Messiah has come and his name is Y'shua." (The ad explained that Y'shua is the Jewish way to say the name of Christ.) The ad is addressed to both gentile and Jew, and offers free books by Moishe Rosen to anyone who does not believe in Y'shua. Because Jews believe that a Jew who follows Christ is no longer a Jew, full page advertisements by Jews who accept Jesus and still claim to be Jewish are disturbing. The second dispute concerns the number of Jewish Christians in America. Jewish opponents of the Messianic Christians claim that there are over 100,000 Jews in America who accept Jesus as the Messiah. Unfortunately numbers are difficult to find because most groups, like Jews for Jesus, do not organize congregations, but send converts to churches where the gospel is preached and where Jewish Christians will feel at home. While some converts might find their way to a Messianic Jewish synagogue, the majority will be integrated into predominantly gentile evangelical conservative Protestant churches. Recently, Jews for Jesus established a congregation in New York City because there was no distinctly Jewish Christian congregation in the area. It remains to be seen whether there will be more churches or whether Jews for Jesus will continue to act as a vestibule for Jewish converts. Moishe Rosen is the executive director of Jews for Jesus which is headquartered in San Francisco.

The most distinctive pieces of literature produced by the Jews for Jesus are their tracts, one-page folded, with a brief eye-catching title. These tracts are freely distributed on street corners and campuses and have been the major vehicle for contacting prospective converts.

1150. Ellegant, Barry. _Growth Book_. San Rafael, CA: Jews for Jesus, 1975. 24pp. Rev. ed.: _Growth Book: Especially for New Jewish Believers_. San Francisco: Jews for Jesus, 1983. 34pp.

1151. -----. _Jews for Jesus_. Plainfield, NJ: Logos International, 1973. 34pp.

1152. Friedman. Bob. _If I Were a Rich Man_. San Rafael, CA: Jews for Jesus, 1977. 14pp.

1153. _Questions and Answers_. San Francisco: Jews for Jesus, 1983.

1154. Rosen, Ceil and Moishe Rosen. _Christ in the Passover_. Chicago: Moody Press, 1978. 112pp.

1155. Rosen, Martin (Moishe Rosen). _How to Witness Simply and Effectively to the Jews_. New York: American Board of Missions to the Jews, 1969. 32pp.

1156. -----. _Our Messianic Mission_. Minneapolis, MN: Messianic Ministries, n.d. 21pp.

1157. Rosen, Moishe. _The Sayings of Chairman Moishe_. Carol Stream, IL: Creation House, 1974. 107pp.

1158. -----. _Y'shua, the Jewish Way to Say Jesus_. Chicago: Moody Press, 1983. 160pp.

1159. -----, and Ceil Rosen. _Share the New Life with a Jew_. Chicago: Moody Press, 1976. 160pp.

1160. ---- with William Procter. _Jews for Jesus_. Old Tappan, NJ: Fleming H. Revell Company, 1974. 126pp.

1161. Rubin, Steffi. _Anti-Semitism_. San Rafael, CA: Jews for Jesus, 1977. 56pp.

1162. Schlamm, Vera, with Bob Friedman. _Pursued_. San Francisco: Hineni Ministries, 1972. 212pp.

1163. Zaretsky, Tuvya. _Turning to God_. Downers Grove, IL: InterVarsity Press, 1985. 29pp.

Tracts
(These tracts have been reprinted and appear under
a variety of imprints. Places of publication include Corte Madera, San Francisco and San Rafael,
California and Skokie, Illinois. Publishers include Jews for Jesus, Jews and Others for Jesus,
and Hineni Ministries.)

1164. Altman, Neil. _Pollution_. n.d.

1165. -----. and Gilda Altman. _Truth, Justice,
Freedom, Peace_. n.d.

1166. -----. _What Is Jewish?_ n.d.

1167. Andrews, Tod. _Love Is a Three Letter Word_.
1976.

1168. Baker, David. _Are You Fa'mished_. 1978.

1169. -----. _Kosher for Passover_. 1982.

1170. _Beware of Jews for Jesus..._ n.d.

1171. Bohlman, Robert. _Have a Nice Day_. 1983

1172. Boker, Pat. _Star Wars_. 1977

1173. -----. _Pac-Man Fever_. 1982.

1174. Chernoff, David. _Roots_. 1977.

1175. Chester, Rivka. _King Kong_. 1977.

1176. -----. _What the World Needs Now_. 1975

1177. Ciavolino, Gina. _Can You Find 36 Michael
Jackson Song Titles in This Pamphlet?_ 1984.

1178. Cohen, Merrill. _Who Needs One More Live
Birth Anyway?_ n.d.

1179. Cross, John. _You've Heard It Said_. 1976.

1180. Dauermann, Naomi. _Red Tape Got You Down_.
1977.

1181. Dauermann, Stuart. *Are You Campus Cause Crazy?* 1981.

1182. -----. *Are You Straight?* n.d.

1183. -----. *The Good Life (Is Not So Good).* 1984.

1184. -----. *Good News and Bad News.* 1985.

1185. -----. *Hula Hoops and Hope.* n.d.

1186. -----. *If You Want It, You Can Get It in New York.* 1984

1187. -----. *Israel or Palestine, Whose Land Is It?* n.d.

1188. Number not used.

1189. -----. *Pornography Is Great...* 1984

1190. Ellegant, Benyomin, *If... You Blame the Jews.* 1977.

1191. -----. *Life Is a Drag.* n.d.

1192. -----. *Wave a Flag.* 1972. Rev., 1984.

1193. -----. *Everybody Loves a Parade.* 1975.

1194. -----. *Fortune-Telling for Fun and Prophet.* 1975.

1195. Fraum, Lee. *Sudden Death Does Not Always Lead to Overtime.* 1983.

1196. Freidel, Jachebed. *Feel Cold Lately.* 1982

1197. Fritz, Jeff. *Training--In a Small Way.* 1981.

1198. Geiser, Steffi. *Everything You Always Wanted to Know about Jesus, But Were Afraid to Ask Your Rabbi.* n.d.

1199. -----. *Everything You Never Wanted to Know about Baruch Goldstein and Were Never Inclined to Ask.* n.d.

1200. -----. <u>Goyim for Jesus</u>. 1974

1201. -----. <u>Heredity? Or Environment?</u> 1972

1202. -----. <u>I Believe With Perfect Faith...</u>
<u>Sometimes</u>. 1972.

1203. -----. <u>If Being Born Hasn't Given You Much</u>
<u>Satisfaction...Try Being Born Again</u>. n.d.

1204. -----. <u>If Life Is a Journey that Means It</u>
<u>Goes Somewhere</u>. 1973

1205. -----. <u>I'm So-So, You're So-So</u>. n.d.

1206. -----. <u>Is Somebody Following Me?</u> 1972.

1207. -----. <u>It's Beginning to Look a Lot Like</u>
<u>Christmas Vacation</u>. Corte Madera, CA: n.d.

1208. -----. <u>Let's Talk Turkey about Thanksgiving</u>.
n.d.

1209. -----. <u>Nostalgia Ain't What It Used to Be...</u>
1974.

1210. -----. <u>Organic Health Foods</u>. 1971

1211. -----. <u>Participation Communication</u>. 1983.

1212. -----. <u>Saved...Schmaved...Who Wants to Be</u>
<u>Saved?</u> 1972.

1213. -----. <u>Science Proves</u>. 1972

1214. -----. <u>Strange Things Are Happening</u>. Corte
Madera, CA: n.d.

1215. -----. <u>Where Was God When the 6 Million</u>
<u>Died</u>. n.d.

1216. -----. <u>Why Things Arn't Working Out</u>. 1973.

1217. ______. <u>Withholding for Fun and Profit!!</u>
1973.

1218. -----. <u>You Oughta Be in Pictures</u>. n.d.

1219. Geiser-Rubin, Steffi. _God's Power, How to Get It, How to Use It_. 1977.

1220. -----. _Subways Are an Underground Movement_. 1974.

1221. Glaser, Mitch. E.T. _A Close Encounter of the Friendly Kind_. 1982.

1222. Number not used.

1223. Goldstein, Baruch. _Good News_. 1973.

1224. -----. _He Can't Possibly Be the Messiah!_ n.d.

1225. -----. _Hey Sport_. 1974.

1226. -----. _Strange Facts About You, God, and Your Mother_. 1984.

1227. _____. _When the Messiah Comes_. 1972.

1228. Goldstein, Marcia. _Ecology_. 1972

1229. Green, Randy. _Investments, Dividends, Interest Rates, and Returns on Your Investments or, How to Be a Financial Wizard_. 1981.

1230. Greenspan, Evan. _Important Cliff Notes_. 1983.

1231. Hevesy, Nikki. _What Will You Be Wearing this Season?_ 1978.

1232. -----. _How to Use Broadsides_. n.d.

1233. -----. _Is It True Jews Don't Believe in Jesus?_ 1972.

1234. _How to Use Broadsides_. n.d.

1235. Jacobs, Loren. _In Case of Nuclear Attack_. 1983.

1236. -----. _Test Your Yiddishkeit_. 1984.

1237. Jacobs, Martha. _Hospital Tsuris_. 1979.

1238. _Jews for Jesus and Your Church_. n.d.

1239. Koenig, Jeffery. _Hide & Seek_. 1975.

1240. -----. _On Hanukkah Don't Forget to Remember_.
1975

1241. -----. _Starvation_. 1975

1242. Korotkin, Shelley. _It's Time to Play School
Again_. Corte Madera, CA: n.d.

1243. -----. _Reincarnation_. 1972.

1244. Kostroff, Mike. _Fame_. 1983.

1245. Kress, Vickie. _Beauty_. Corte Madera, CA:
n.d.

1246. -----. _If Being Born Hasn't Given You Much
Satisfaction, Try Being Born Again_. 1971.

1247. -----. _Long Long Ago There Was a Patriotic
Prophet_. Corte Madera, CA: n.d.

1248. -----. _Subways Aren't Much Fun_. n.d.

1249. Kroupa, Carol. _Life Used to Be So Simple_.
n.d.

1250. Kugler, Irving D. _Are you a Shlemiel or a
Shlimazel?_ 1977.

1251. Levine, Dan. _The Law and the Prophets at the
Flatbush Yeshiva_.

1252. Lusk, Ron. _Torah Is Good for the Soul_. 1984.

1253. -----. _You Can Have Beautiful Feet_. 1977.

1254. Maass, Eliezer. _Airport `78_. 1977.

1255. -----. _Why a Buck?_ 1983.

1256. Mendelsohn, Bob. _The Story of Joannie & Save
the Whales_. 1980.

1257. Millenson, Jeffrey. _Do You Need Two Faces?_

1258. Miller, Rich. _If You Want to Handle Life Without Drugs_. n.d.

1259. Minsk, Alan. _I Thought Life Should Make Some Kind of Sense_. n.d.

1260. Moskowitz, Jh'an. _All the World Is a Stage_. 1975.

1261. -----. _If Easter is a Jewish Holiday, I Must Be an Egg!!_ n.d.

1262. -----. _Signs_. 1984.

1263. -----. _To Be or Not to Be_. 1984.

1264. Moss, Joshua. _How to Combat the Missionaries--Some Advice from Jews for Jesus_. 1984.

1265. Nadler, Sam. _How to Get Thru_. n.d.

1266. -----. _Jesus Makes Us Sing Jewish Songs_. n.d.

1267. -----. _Pardon Me But..._ 1982.

1268. -----. _Washington Slept Here_. 1973.

1269. -----. _You Don't Have to Be Jewish to Love Jesus_. 1977.

1270. Perlman, Susan. _The Gay Life_. n.d.

1271. -----. _If Jesus Is the Messiah...Why?_ 1978.

1272. -----. _Jews Should Not Believe in Jesus... Unless..._ 1984.

1273. -----. _Mary Hartman, Mary Hartman_. 1976.

1274. -----. _On the First Day of Christmas My Rabbi Gave to Me..._ 1978.

1275. -----. _The Sequel to End All Sequels_. 1983.

1276. -----. <u>Some People Don't Believe in God</u>. n.d.

1277. Rabinovitz, Amy. <u>Auld Lang Shlep</u>. Corte Madera, CA: n.d.

1278. -----. <u>The Christmas I</u>. 1972.

1279. -----. <u>Who Ever Heard of a Jewish Priest</u>. 1978.

1280. Richman, Kresha. <u>Tourist Truris</u>. 1975.

1281. Robinson, Rich. <u>Return of the Jedi</u>. 1983.

1282. -----. <u>Want to Buy a Home Computer</u>. 1984.

1283. Rosen, Ceil. <u>The Age of Aquarius</u>. n.d.

1284. -----. <u>The Liberated Woman</u>. Corte Madera, CA: n.d.

1285. -----. <u>Then I Met Messiah</u>. n.d.

1286. -----. <u>What Is Your Sign</u>. 1972.

1287. Rosen, Moishe. <u>And Thou Shalt Call His Name Y'shua</u>. 1982

1288. -----. <u>Are You a Peacemaking Orphan?</u> Corte Madera, CA: n.d.

1289. -----. <u>Black Is Beautiful</u>. n.d.

1290. -----. <u>Brotherhood Weak</u>. n.d.

1291. -----. <u>Christmas Is a Jewish Holiday</u>. 1970

1292. -----. <u>Dear D-Doctor</u>. Corte Madera, CA: n.d.

1293. -----. <u>Doing the Beautiful Thing</u>. 1972.

1294. -----. <u>Everybody Needs a Chance</u>. 1972.

1295. -----. <u>Evolution</u>. n.d.

1296. -----. <u>Fortune-Telling for Fun and Prophet</u>. n.d.

1297. -----. <u>A God By Any Other Name...</u> 1972

1298. -----. <u>Graduate</u>. 1972

1299. -----. <u>Haman Didn't Like Jews</u>. 1972

1300. -----. <u>Happy Yom Kippur</u>. 1972.

1301. -----. <u>Hey You</u>. 1975.

1302. -----. <u>Hitching</u>. n.d.

1303. Number not used.

1304. -----. <u>If You Are Elected</u>. 1984.

1305. -----. <u>An Important Announcment from the People Who Brought You Jesus</u>. 1980.

1306. -----. <u>Is It True Jews Don't Believe in Jesus?</u> n.d.

1307. -----. <u>It's No Fun</u>. Corte Madsera, CA: n.d.

1308. -----. <u>It's Not Like</u>. 1983.

1309. -----. <u>Jesus Made Me Kosher</u>. 1971.

1310. -----. <u>Jesus Was a Prophet, But...</u> n.d.

1311. -----. <u>Jews for Jesus</u>. 1971.

1312. -----. <u>Jews for Jesus, What Do They Believe</u>. Corte Madera, CA: n.d.

1313. -----. <u>Kosher Pigs</u>. Corte Madera, CA: n.d.

1314. _____. <u>A Message from a Meshumad</u>. 1972.

1315. -----. <u>A Message from Squares</u>. Corte Madera, CA: n.d.

1316. -----. <u>Mother Love</u>. n.d.

1317. -----. <u>Only One Winner in This Race</u>. Corte Madera, CA: n.d.

1318. -----. <u>Once There Was a Freak</u>. n.d.

1319. -----. <u>Passover</u>. Corte Madera, CA: N.d.

1320. -----. <u>Peace Isn't Nothing</u>. Corte Madera, CA: 1971.

1321. -----. <u>Promises, Promises, Promises, That Won't Be Broken</u>. 1976.

1322. -----. <u>The Rat Race</u>. 1983.

1323. -----. <u>Shalom</u>. 1984.

1324. -----. <u>Test Your Tolerance</u>. 1982.

1325. -----. <u>Voting Makes You Think</u>. Corte Madera, CA: n.d.

1326. -----. <u>Welcome Atheists</u>. 1983.

1327. -----. <u>What's a Nice Person Like You</u>. Corte Madera, CA: n.d.

1328. -----. <u>Who or What Is Jews for Jesus</u>. 1985.

1329. -----. <u>Why You Are Important</u>. 1984.

1330. -----. <u>Will Israel Survive?</u> 1974.

1331. -----, and S. Geiser. <u>Justice</u>. 1972

1332. Rosen, Ruth. <u>I Don't Believe in Proselying</u>. 1984.

1333. -----. <u>Keeping Cool</u>. 1981.

1334. -----. <u>The Passover Plot</u>. ????

1335. Rosenblum, Larry. <u>I Want Proof</u>. 1978.

1336. Rubin, Barry. <u>Junk Food</u>. 1978.

1337. Rubin, Reuben. <u>Transcendental Meditation Will Not Solve All Your Problems</u>. 1974.

1338. Rubin, Steffi. <u>Arson Burns Us Up!</u> 1978.

1339. -----. <u>Let's Talk Turkey About Thanksgiving</u>.

1973.

1340. Sacks, Herschel. <u>Are You a Sound Freak?</u>
1977.
1341. Sacks, Wendy. <u>Scared of the Dark</u>. 1977.

1342. Schiffman, Robyn. <u>Israel--A Sign of the</u>
<u>Times</u>. 1982.

1343. Schriebman, Elinor. <u>You Get What You Pay</u>
<u>For, Or Do You?</u> 1972.

1344. ------. <u>You've Come a Long Way Baby!</u> n.d.

1345. Sieger, Matt. <u>It's Only a Crutch</u>. 1981

1346. ------. <u>They Did It Again! Superbowl 1985</u>.

1347. Silverman, Rachmiel. <u>The "____" Shall Rise</u>
<u>Again</u>. 1976.

1348. Skoropinski, Bruce. <u>Give My Regards to</u>
<u>Broadway</u>. 1983

1349. ------. <u>Inflation</u>. 1972.

1350. Smoot, John Murray. <u>Jesus Was Not a</u>
<u>Christian</u>. 1979.

1351. Snyder, Avi. <u>Practice Makes Perfect</u>. 1979.

1352. Steiner, Paul. <u>Run for Your Life</u>. 1983.

1353. Straus, Cyndi. <u>Will Jeans Last Forever</u>.
1983.

1354. Strobbe, Laura. <u>Caution Toxic Waste</u>. 1983.

1355. <u>Where Was God When the 6 Million Died?</u>
1981.

1356. Winter, Mottel. <u>Order</u>. 1972.

1357. ------. <u>Valentine's Day</u>. 1973.

1358. Zaretsky, Tuvya. <u>Jesus for Jews</u>. 1977.

1359. ------. <u>Moses for Jesus</u>. 1982.

1360. -----. <u>The Star Trek Fantasy</u>. 1979.

1361. -----. <u>What's a Four-letter Word You Can Say to God's Face?</u> n.d.

Periodicals

1362. <u>Newsletter</u>. 60 Haight Street, San Francisco, CA 94102-5895

1363. <u>Issues</u>. Box 11250, San Francisco, CA 94101

Christian and Secular Reactions to the Jews for Jesus

1364. "Billy Graham Described as One of the Greatest Friends of Jews." <u>The Jewish Weke American Examiner</u> (March 28, 1983) 36.

1365. Buursma, Bruce. "Jews, Christians at Crossroads." <u>Chicago Tribune</u> (November 28, 1982) 16.

1366. Forbes, Cheryl. "Something There Is That Doesn't Like a Wall." <u>Christianity Today</u> (April 26, 1974) 874-75.

1367. Gelwick, Richard. "Will the Jesus Revolution Revive Anti-Semitism?" <u>Christian Century</u> (May 10, 1972) 545-48.

1368. LaMagdeleine, Donald R. <u>Jews for Jesus: Organizational Structure and Supporters</u>. Berkeley: Graduate Theological Union, M. A. Thesis, 1977.

1369. Mano, D. Keith. "Jews for Jesus". <u>National Review</u> (September 30, 1977) 1126-1127.

1370. Miller, Lindsay. "Jews as 'Jesus Freaks.'" <u>New York Post</u> (September 2, 1972).

1371. Murphy, Lyle. "Questions and Answers about Jews for Jesus." <u>Voice</u> (September-October 1977) 5-6.

1372. Rosen, Martin M. "Why Are Young Jews Turning to Christ." <u>Christianity Today</u> (November 10, 1972) 124-125

1373. Rosen, Moishe. "Dialogue, Evangelism and the Jewish Community." <u>Presbyterian Guardian</u> (September 1978). Reprinted as 4-page flyer.

1374. -----. "How a Jew Became a Goy." <u>Life and Faith</u> (December 7, 1974) 12.

1375. -----, with William Procter. "Jews for Jesus." <u>Christian Review</u> (September-October 1974) 10-11.

B. The Messianic Jewish Movement

In essence, Messianic Jews are individuals who believe in Jesus Christ as Lord and Savior and practice the Christian faith, while wishing to retain an identity on a cultural level with the Jewish community and on a "national" level with Israel. The movement, which emerged in the early 1970s, grew out of a old argument within the Hebrew Christian community over the role of missionary organizations and the "gentilization" process usually undergone by new converts from Judaism to Christianity. Most early leaders, who spearheaded Jewish missions, denounced any attempts to build a distinctly Jewish Christianity. There were, however, always minority voices. During the 1970s, within the larger context of the Jews for Jesus movement, and the articulation of Jewish converts as "completed Jews," a new burst of Messianic Judaism appeared. Observers saw its first manifestation in the Young Hebrew Christian Alliance of America, an affiliate of the Hebrew Christian Alliance of America. Outsiders began to take the movement seriously after the younger members captured the Hebrew Christian Alliance and changed its name to Messianic Jewish Alliance of America. The International Hebrew Christian Alliance also became a part of the movement and soon, as messianic congregations were formed around the United States, a Union of Messianic Congregations was added as a third major structure. Like much of evangelical Christianity, particular leaders such as Mike Evans and Sid Roth developed a variety of independent publications and ministries. David Rausch (1390-92) has become the major chronicler of the new movement which is still experiencing first generation growing pains.

General Sources

1376. Adams, Blair. _The Messianics: Converting Jews to Paganism or Gentiles to Judaism?_ The Author, 1976. 10pp.

1377. Coote, Robert T. "How Kosher Can Christianity Get?" _Eternity_ (September 1975). 15-17, 24-27.

1378. Frydland, Rachmiel. _Joy Cometh in the Morning_. Chattanooga, TN: Messianic Fellowship, Tennessee Temple Schools, 1972. 52pp.

1379. -----. When Being Jewish Was a Crime.
Nashville, TN: Thomas Nelson, 1978. 166pp.

1380. Glass, Arthur E. And His Name Shall Be
Called Wonderful. Chattanooga, TN: Southern
Mesianic Witness to Israel, 1946. 48pp.

1381. -----. Yeshua in the Tenach. Augusta, GA:
The Author, n.d. 8pp.

1382. -----. Why I Believe. Los Angeles: Peace
and Truth Seekers, n.d. 6pp.

1383. Goble, Phillip E. Everything You Need to
Grow a Messianic Synagogue. South Pasadena, CA:
William Carey Library, 1974. 158pp.

1384. Goldberg, Louis. "The Messianic Jew."
Christianity Today 18 (February 1, 1974) 6-11.

1385. Hefley, James C. The New Jews. Wheaton,
IL: Tyndale House Publishers, 1971. 158pp

1386. Hort, Fenton J. Judaistic Christianity: A
Course of Lectures. Grand Rapids: Baker Book
House, 1980.

1387. Hutchens, James W. A Case for Messianic
Judaism. Pasadena, CA: Fuller Theological
Seminary, D.Miss. dissertation, 1874.

1388. -----. "Messianic Judaism: A Progress
Report." Missiology 5 (July 1977) 285-99.

1389. Joffe, Bruce H. "Jews Who Believe in
Jesus." Christianity Today (July 13, 1984) 16-21.

1390. Rausch, David A. "Jews Against 'Messianic'
Jews." In Herbert Richardson, ed. New Religions &
Mental Health: Understanding the Issues. New
York: Edwin Mellen Press, 1980. Pp. 39-47.

1391. -----. "Jews Evangelized, Messianic Jews."
Midstream 23, 2 (February 1977) 36-41.

1392. -----. Messianic Judaism: Its History,
Theology, and Polity. New York: Edwin Mellen
Press, 1982. 283pp.

1393. Tamarkin, Civia. "The Jews Who Walk with
Jesus." Chicago Tribune Magazine (November 19,
1978) 44-48, 52-54.

1394. Willoughby, William, "A Breakthrough for Messianic Judaism." <u>Moody Monthly</u> (March 1972). Rept.: 1977. 6pp.

Periodicals

1395. <u>"Hashivah," The Return</u>. %Friends of Zion, Box 432, Northridge, CA 91328-0432

1396. <u>The Messianic Outreach</u>. Box 37062, Cincinnati, OH 45222.

1397. <u>The Shofar Shalom</u>. %Beth Ha Shofar, 13001 37th Avenue So., Seattle, WA 98168.

1. Opposition to Messianic Judaism from Within the Hebrew Christian Movement

The desire to develop a form of Christianity which retains the cultural and religious elements of Judaism has emerged periodically during the twentieth century throughout the larger Hebrew Christian movement. David Baron was an early opponent of the tendency which was effectively fought until the 1970s. In the midst of the rise of Messianic Judaism, the American Messianic Association has provided the most vocal opposition. Along with articles in its periodical, it has reprinted the earlier work by Baron and one tract by its executive director.

1398. Baron, David. <u>"Messianic Judaism"; or Judaising Christianity</u>. Chicago: American Messianic Fellowship, n.d. 16 pp. Reprinted from <u>The Scattered Nation</u>, October 1911.

1399. Gade, Ralph M. <u>What Is Messianic Judaism?</u> Chicago: American Association for Jewish Evangelism, n.d. 3pp.

2. Messianic Jewish Alliance of America (formerly: Hebrew Christian Alliance of America)

The first attempt to form the Hebrew Christian Alliance took place in 1903 in Mountain Lake Park, Maryland. Many people feared that such an alliance was divisive and would lead to the formation of a separate Hebrew Christian church.

Consequently, the alliance did not succeed until 1915, at which time it began a program of evangelism and published a journal, <u>The Alliance Quarterly</u>. In its first year, <u>The Alliance Quarterly</u> raised one of the most controversial ideas among Hebrew Christians in this century. It condemned the idea that a Jew could become a Christian and still continue to observe any Jewish customs or rituals. The attack was quite effective. In spite of dissenting voices throughout its history, the alliance prevented the emergence of Messianic Judaism until the 1970s. Baptist pastor S. B. Rohold was its first president. Prominent for many years, Arthur W. Kac served as its president from 1956 to 1961. In more recent years Aaron Klingerman and Rachmiel Frydland have held that post.

In the early 1960s, Manny Brotman, a graduate of the Jewish studies program of the Moody Bible Institute in Chicago, formed Shalom, a ministry in Chicago which offered a free New Testament and a Bible correspondence course to potential Jewish converts, and a "Young" Hebrew Christian Alliance as a branch of the Alliance. Brotman, with Joe and Debbie Finkelstein and Sandra Sheskin, preached the gospel to confused young people who were searching for answers in drugs and in uninhibited life styles. In Messianic Judaism, young Jews found a way to reject what their parents stood for while, at the same time, often becoming even more Jewish. These "Young" Hebrew Christians with their distinctive Messianic Judaism soon outnumbered the older members of the Hebrew Christian Alliance. In 1975, after an aborted effort in 1973, the young members won the vote at the Conference of the Hebrew Christian Alliance and changed the name to the Messianic Jewish Alliance. The organization is headquartered in Haverton, Pennsylvania.

(Note: Authors affiliated with the Alliance prior to 1970 may or may not support its present position regarding Messianic Judaism. Some leaders withdrew after the changes in 1975.)

1400. Brotman, Manny. <u>How to Share Messiah</u>. Washington, D.C.: Messianic Jewish Movement International, 1972.

1401. ------. <u>The Jewish Bible Approach</u>. Washington, D.C.: Messianic Jewish Movement International, 1972.

1402. Buksbazen, Victor. _The Hebrew Christian and Israel_. Chicago: Hebrew Christian Alliance of America, 16pp.

1403. -----. _Who Crucified Him?_ Chicago: Hebrew Christian Alliance of America, n.d. 12pp.

1404. Finklestein, Joseph. _Jewish Holidays, A Study Guide_. Washington, D.C.: Messianic Jewish Movement International.

1405. Gair, Bernard J., ed. _The Gospel and the Jew: Some Collected Papers of Aaron J. Klingerman_. Privately Published, n.d.

1406. -----. _I Am a Completed Jew_. New York: New York Mission to the Jews. 8pp.

1407. Gartenhaus, Jacob. _Come Now, Let Us Reason Together_. Chicago: Hebrew Christian Alliance of America, n.d. 18pp.

1408. -----. _How to Win the Jews_. Chicago: Hebrew Christian Alliance of America, 1963. 15pp.

1409. Grace, Roy. _The Christian Debt_. Chicago: Hebrew Christian Alliance of America, n.d. 10pp.

1410. Juster, Daniel. _Jewishness and Jesus_. Downers Gove, IL: Intervarsity Christian Press, 1977.

1411. -----. _True Dialog: A Challenge to Fellow Jews Concerning the Messiah_. Chicago: Messianic Jewish Alliance of America, 1977.

1412. Kac, Arthur. _Can a Jew Become a Follower of Jesus Christ and Remain a Jew?_ Chicago: Hebrew Christain Alliance of America, n.d. 24pp.

1413. -----. _The Death and Resurrection of Israel_. Baltimore, MD: King Brothers, 1969. 239pp.

1414. -----. _The Messiahship of Jesus_. Chicago: Moody Press, 1980. 351pp. Rev. ed. Grand Rapids, MI: Baker Book House, 1986. 352pp.

1415. -----. _The Messianic Hope_. Grand Rapids, MI: Baker Book House, 1975. 353pp.

1416. -----. _The Rebirth of the State of Israel_. Chicago: Moody Press, 1958. 386pp.

1417. -----. <u>The Spiritual Condition of the Jewish People</u>. Grand Rapids, MI: Baker Book House, 1983. 153pp.

1418. Klingeman, Aaron Judah. <u>Feasts & Fasts in Israel</u>. Baltimore: Emmanuel Neighborhood House, n.d.

1419. -----. <u>The Gospel and the Jews</u>. Baltimore: King Brothers, 1969. 205pp.

1420. -----. <u>Our Triune God</u>. Chicago: Hebrew Christian Alliance of America, n.d. 15pp.

1421. ----. <u>Sharing Christ with Our Jewish Neighbors</u>. New York: Board of National Missions, n.d. 15pp. Rept.: Chicago: Hebrew Christian Alliance of America, n.d. 15pp.

1422. -----. "Sukkoth, the Feast of Tabernacles." <u>The Alliance Witness</u> (October 16, 1963).

1423. -----. <u>The Trinity</u>. Asheville, NC: Jewish Neighbor Evangelism, n.d. 19pp.

1424. -----. <u>We Have Found the Messiah</u>. Chicago: Hebrew Christian Alliance of America, n.d. 15pp.

1425. Liberman, Paul. <u>The Fig Tree Blossoms</u>. Harrison, AK: Fountain Press, 1976. 123pp.

1426. Machlin, A. B. <u>Are You a Real Jew?</u> Chicago: Hebrew Christian Alliance of America, n.d. 20pp.

1427. <u>Questionaire, "To the Jew First."</u> Chicago: Hebrew Christian Alliance of America, n.d. 4pp.

1428. Rohold, S. R.. <u>The War and the Jew</u>. Toronto: Macmillian Conpany of Canada. 1915. 97pp.

1429. Stone, Nathan J. <u>What Year Is It?</u> Chicago: Hebrew Christian Alliance of America, n.d. 10pp.

1430. Tamarkkin, Civia. "The Jews Who Walk with Jesus." <u>Chicago Tribune Magazine</u> (November 19, 1978) 44-48, 52, 54.

1431. Zutrau, Morris. <u>The Virgin Birth</u>. Hebrew Christian Alliance of America, n.d. 15pp.

1432. <u>The American Messianic Jew</u>. 1445 City Line Avenue, #9B, Philadelphia, PA 19151 (Supercedes <u>The American Messianic Jewish Quarterly</u> (1975-1983) and <u>The American Hebrew Christian</u> (1916-1975). The fiftieth anniversary issue (Spring 1965) devoted significant space to a series of historical articles concerning the Alliance.)

1433. <u>The Shalom Challenge</u>. Chicago, 1963- ?

3. International Hebrew Christian Alliance

Founded largely through the efforts of Mark John Levy in 1925 in London, the International Hebrew Christian Alliance attempted to bring together the work of the Hebrew Christian Alliance of America and its counterpart in other countries and Great Britain. It has pioneered Christian Jewish missions internationally. Levy was one of the first to warn against gentilization of Christian Jews, continuing the controversy that would become dominant in the alliance in the 1970s. The alliance stands behind the organization of the first truly Hebrew Christian church in 1934. This successful church, the First Hebrew Christian Presbyterian Church of Chicago, was organized by David Bronstein, Sr.

In 1962, David Bronstein, Jr. was called to head the International Hebrew Christian Alliance. The alliance currently has affiliated alliances in 16 countries including Israel, where it maintains a home for the aged and has a number of congregations. Their publication, the <u>Living Scriptures</u>, a Messianic Jewish edition of the Bible, is in widespread use among the Messianic congregations. Even though the Bronsteins were pioneers in the Messianic movement, a more controversial approach than integration into gentile churches, they were accepted because they maintained a low profile and did not establish many congregations. Instead, the International Hebrew Christian Alliance gathered existing Jewish congregations into a worldwide organization. Its current president is H. Herz-Hablutzel, the American secretary is David Bronstein, Jr., and the American headquarters are in Palm Harbor, Florida.

1434. Benhayim, Menahem. "The Remnant in Israel Today." _Christianity Today_ (January 21, 1983) 12-15.

1435. Bronstein, Sr., David. _Does a Jew Need to be Converted?_ N.p.: n.d. 16pp.

1436. -----. _The Jewish Passover and the Christian Community_. Chicago: The Author, 1941. 30pp.

1437. ------. _Judaism and Christianity: Are They the Same?_ Clearwater, FL: O'Neill, Oliver, MacKenzie, Inc. 1963. 121pp.

1438. -----. _Peniel Portrait_. Chicago: D. Cameron Peck, 1943. 110pp.

1439. -----. _The Relationship of Judaism and Christianity_. N.p.: n.d. 8pp.

1440. -----. _What and Why?_ Chicago: First Hebrew Christian Church, n.d. 12pp.

1441. Levy, Mark John. _Christianity, the Flower and Fruit of Judaism_. Washington, DC: Christian League of Jewish Friendship, 1923.

1442. -----. _Some Thoughts on Life's Battles_. Louisville, KY: J. P. Morton & Co., 1888. 117pp.

1443. -----. _13, the National Number in the United States_. Washington, DC: Christian League of Jewish Friendship, [1924]. 20pp.

1444. -----. _To the Jews and Christians of America_. Washington, DC: R. H. Darby, n.d. [189_?]. 15pp.

1445. -----. _Workings of an English Christian Heart_. London: Operative Jewish Converts, 1892. 143pp.

1446. _Living for the Messiah_. Clearwater, FL: International Hebrew Christian Alliance, n.d. 6pp.

1447. _Peniel's Ministry Invites You_. Chicago: Peniel Community Center, n.d. 12pp.

1448. _What It Is...What It Does..._ Palm Harbor, FL: International Hebrew Christian Allaince, n.d. 8pp.

Periodical

1449. <u>The Hebrew Christian</u>. %Shalom, Brockenhurst
Road, Ramsgate CT11 8ED, England

4. Union of Messianic Congregations

John Foscher, formerly with the American
Messianic Fellowship, until he broke with that
organization over the messianic question, is
prominent in both the Union of Messianic Congregations and the International Hebrew Christian
Alliance, for which he has served as the deputy
secretary in America.

1450. Fischer, John. <u>His Ambassadors to His
People</u>. Chicago: American Messianic Fellowship,
[1974 ?]. 62pp.

1451. -----. <u>Sharing Israel's Messiah</u>. Highland
Park, IL: Watchman Association, 1978. Rept. as:
<u>The Olive Tree Connection</u>. Downers Grove, IL: In-
terVarsity Press, 1983. 209pp.

1452. Juster, Daniel. <u>Jewishness and Jesus</u>.
Downers Grove, IL: InterVarsity Press, 1977.

1453. -----. <u>True Dialog: A Challenge to Fellow
Jews Concerning the Messiah</u>. Chicago: Messianic
Jewish Alliance of America, 1977.

5. Mike Evans Ministries

Mike Evans, a Pentecostal believer, has developed
an independent Messianic ministry headquartered
in Texas. His first book (1459) chronicled the
emergence of the movement.

1454. Evans, Mike. <u>Israel, America's Key to
Survival</u>. Bedford, TX: Bedford Books, 1983.
138pp.

1455. -----. <u>Israel, the Middle East and the
Great Powers</u>. Jerusalem: Shikmona Publishers,
1984.

1456. -----. <u>Jerusalem D. C.</u> Bedford, TX: Bedford Books, 1984. 162pp.

1457. -----. <u>Let My People Go!</u> Nashville, TN: Nelson Resource Management, 1985. 104pp.

1458. -----. <u>The Return</u>. Nashville, TN: Thomas Nelson Publishers, 1986. 236pp.

1459. -----. <u>Young Lions of Judah</u>. Plainfield, NJ: Logos International, 1974. 116pp.

1460. <u>Yeshua Hamashiach</u>. Dallas/Ft. Worth, TX: Wisdom House Publishers, 1973. 32pp.

Periodical

1461. <u>Middle East News Alert</u>. Box 709, Bedford, TX 76021

6. Messianic Vision

The Messianic Vision is a ministry built around the radio ministry in the Washington, D.C. area of Sid Roth. He has become a popular speaker at the annual gatherings of the Messianic Jewish Alliance of America.

1462. Roth, Sid. <u>Something for Nothing</u>. Plainfield, NJ: 20505, International, 1976. 133pp.

1463. <u>Why God?</u> Bethesda, MD: Messianic Vision, n.d. 16pp.

Periodical

1464. <u>The Messianic Vision Newsletter</u>. Box 34444, Washington, DC 20034

JEWISH RESPONSES TO HEBREW CHRISTIANITY

A. General Opposition to Conversion

The Jewish community has a centuries-long history of opposition to various attempts by Christian organizations to proselytize Jews. Many leaders have seen such Jewish missionary activity as a direct threat to the survival of Judaism. During the twentieth century, major strides have been taken by the leading congregational and rabbinical organizations to change the basic relationship between the two communities so that dialogue replaces any organized strategy aimed at the conversion of Jews. As a result of that effort, most of the larger Christian bodies have withdrawn support from such missions and their missionary departments have abandoned missionary programs which target the Jewish community.

Meanwhile, the presence of independent fundamentalist and evangelical Jewish Christian missionary groups, some continuations of abandoned denominational programs, in steadily increasing numbers through the century, have led to sporadic efforts to counter their effectiveness. Jewish interest in countering such groups have led, for example, to the only real historical writing, however polemic, concerning American Jewish missionary efforts.

Jewish missions blossomed after the establishment of the state of Israel. Most of these followed traditional missionary patterns and as a result did not cause a significant reaction within the Jewish community. Then, during the early 1970s, some rabbis began to recognize a more aggressive pattern centered upon what was to become Jews for Jesus. That alarm became focused in 1973 because of the national evangelical thrust by a coalition of evangelical Christians popularly known as Key 73. Jewish leaders moved quickly to mobilize elements of the Christian community (primarily Roman Catholics and liberal Protestants) to denounce any targeting of the Jewish community, and to organize the Jewish community to resist any proselytizing programs conducted in their midst.

The opposition to Key 73 which on the one hand led to the establishment of formal dialogues between Jewish and evangelical leaders also alerted Jewish leaders to attempts of a wide variety of groups, Christian and non-Christian, to convert Jews. Specifically, rabbis and others began to denounce cultic groups, some of which were believed to have a large percentage of Jews among their members and many of which had Jews in prominent leadership positions. The broad attempt to program against conversionist groups is clearly seen in such volumes as Daum (1477), developed as curriculum for Reform Jewish synagogues. In general, orthodox Christian, peripherally Christian and non-Christian groups which had visible evangelical techniques were considered as one force opposing the Jewish community. In Jewish thought, Christian missions became strongly associated with the cult phenomena (1480, 1491).

Among the Jewish missionary groups, the Jews for Jesus were singled out as the most significant of the more than one hundred Jewish missionary agencies functioning in America. This targeting of the Jews for Jesus is an indication of its effectiveness and its impressive growth from its original center in California to a presence in most urban areas across the United States. However, its growth is only part of the reason for concern by Jewish leaders. They have reacted strongly to the Jews for Jesus argument that Jewish converts to Christianity can still be considered Jews, "completed Jews." That concept, which led directly to the Messianic Movement and the establishment of Christian Messianic synagogues both offended Jewish ideals and brought forth charges of deception upon Messianic leaders.

The literature in reaction to Christian missionary efforts has been vast, indicative of the seriousness with which the Jewish community has considered the issue. The items listed below include the recent books and a representative selection of articles on the topic. They cover the range of perspectives from the most militant aggressive form of response (which would include deprogramming) to those who would advocate a more defensive and protective form based in the education of Jews and alerting them to missionary activity in their neighborhood.

1465. Adler, Moshe. "Alienation and Jewish Jesus Freajs." _Judaism_ 23 (1974) 287-97.

1466. Adler, Rachel. "The Concept of Messiah in Jewish Tradition." _Davka_ 2, 2 (March-April 1972) 2-6.

1467. Berger, David and Michael Wyschograd. _Jews and Jewish Christianity_. New York: KTAV Publishing House, 1978. 71pp.

1468. Birnholtz, R. J. "Jewish Assertiveness in Combating Missionaries." _Jewish Digest_ 24 (November 1978) 18-23.

1469. Brickner, Balfour. "Christian Missionaries and a Jewish Response." _Worldview_ 21, 5 (May 1978) 37-41.

1470. "Christian Mission and Jewish Witness." Special issue of _Face to Face_ (New York) 3-4 (Fall-Winter 1977). 32pp.

1471. Cohen, Esther. "Jews for Jesus: One Jew's Response." _Christianity and Crisis_ (November 13, 1978) 278-80.

1472. Cohen, Mark. "Missionaries in Our Midst:

The Appeal of Alternatives." _Analysis_ (Washington, D.C.) 64 (March 1978) 1-8.

1473. Cohen, Robert A. "Infiltrating the 'Jews for Jesus.'" _St. Louis Jewish Light_ 33, 25 (1978). Condensed version: _Jewish Digest_ (February 1979) 8-12.

1474. Cohon, Samuel S. "How Christian Mission Feels to a Jew." _The Christian Century_ (December 6, 1933) 1530-32.

1475. -----. "The Jew and Christian Evangelism." _International Review of Missions_ 22, 88 (October 1933) 470-80. (Also see the responding article by Edwyn Bevan.)

1476. "Considerations on the Jewish Complaint Regarding Christian Propaganda Among Jews." _International Review of Missions_ 22, 88 (October 1933) 481-99.

1477. Daum, Annette. _Missionary and Cult Movements_. New York: Department of Interreligious Affairs, 1977. 78pp.

1478. Eichhorn, David Max. _Evangelizing the American Jew_. Middle Village, NY: Jonathan David Publishers, 1978. 210pp.

1479. -----. "Hebrew Christianity." _Jewish Spectator_ 41 (Fall 1976) 33-35.

1480. Fisch, Dov Aharoni. _Jews for Nothing_. New York: Feldheim Publishers, 1984. 368pp.

1481. Fishman, Samuel Z. "Jewish 'Jesus Freaks.'" _The Jewish Digest_ 18, 7, (April 1973) 1-3.

1482. Freuder, Samuel. _A Missionary's Return to Judaism_. New York: The Sinai Publishing Company, 1915. 203pp. Rev. ed. as: _My Return to Judaism_. 1922.

1483. Friedman, Theodore. _Evangelicals-Are They Good for the Jews?_ Palm Beach, FL: Anti-Defamation League of B'nai B'rith, 1978. 12 page typescript.

1484. -----. "Religious Cults: How Serious a Danger?" <u>ADL Bulletin</u> 34, 4 (April 1977) 12.

1485. Gittelsohn, Roland B. "Jews for Jesus--Are They for Real?" <u>Midstream</u> 23, 2 (February 1979) 41-45.

1486. Glazerson, M. <u>From Hinduism Back to Christianity</u>. Los Angeles: Himelsein, Glazerson Publishers, 1984. 117pp.

1487. Gutman, Ernest. <u>The Hebrew-Christians</u>. Philadelphia: Dorrance Company, 1973.

1488. Gutwirth, Jacques. "Jews Among Evangelists in Los Angeles." <u>The Jewish Journal of Sociology</u> 14 (Summer 1982) 39-55.

1489. "The Hebrew Bible Misconstrued." <u>Reconstructionist</u> 49, 9 (December 1973) 16-21.

1490. Hecht, Shea and Chaim Clorfene. <u>Confessions of a Jewish Cultbuster</u>. Brooklyn, NY: Tosefos Media, Inc., 1985. 244pp.

1491. Jacobs, Steven. "How to Answer the Christian Missionary." <u>Jewish Digest</u> 21 (September 1975) 14-17.

1492. Kaplan, Aryeh. <u>The Real Messiah?</u> New York: National Conference of Synagogue Youth, 1976. 106pp.

1493. Kripke, Myer S. "Letter to a Kind Lady." <u>The Christian Century</u> (November 28, 1973) 1172-73.

1494. Lasker, Daniel J. <u>Jewish Philosophical Polemics Against Christianity in the Middle Ages</u>. New York: Ktav, 1977. 286pp.

1495. Levine, Samuel. <u>You Take Jesus, I'll Take God</u>. Los Angeles: Homorah Press, 1980. 134pp.

1496. Luxenberg, Stan. "The Soul Snatchers of Long Island." <u>Moment</u> 2 (May 1977) 7-10.

1497. Mirsky, Norman B. "The Jesus Jew."
<u>Reconstructionist</u> 49, 9 (December 1973) 11-16.

1498. Mitchell, Elichai and Shrira Lindsey. "Jews
Do Believe in Jesus." <u>Davka</u> 2, 2 (March-April
1972) 7-17.

1499. Neubauer, Adolf and S. R. Driver. <u>The
Fifty-Third Chapter of Isaiah According to Jewish
Interpreters</u>. New York: KTAV, 1969. 2 Vols.

1500. Packouz, Kalman. <u>How to Stop an
Intermarriage</u>. Jerusalem: Intermarriage Crises
Conference, 1976. 159pp.

1501. Rudin, A. James and Marcia. "Onward
(Hebrew) Christian Soldiers." <u>Present Tense</u> 4, 4
(Summer 1977) 17-26.

1502. Sherman, Shlomah. <u>Escape from Jesus</u>. Mount
Vernon, NY: Decalogue Books, 1983. 223pp.

1503. Shuman, Albert M. <u>The Religious Heritage of
America</u>. San Diego: A. S. Barnes & Company, 1981.
See pp. 415-16.

1504. Silverman, Lawrence M. <u>What to Say When a
Missionary Comes to Your Door</u>. Plymouth, MA: Congregation Beth Jacob, n.d. 5pp.

1505. Sobel, B. Z. <u>Hebrew Christianity: The Thirteenth Tribe</u>. New York: John Wiley & Sons, 1974.
413pp.

1506. Ungar, Andre. "Jews and Jesus Freaks."
<u>Reconstructionist</u> 49, 9 (December 1973) 7-11.

1507. Urofsky, M. I. "Does Jesus Make You
Kosher?" <u>Jewish Observer</u> 26 (September 1, 1977).

1507a. Weiss-Rosmarin, Trude."Did Jesus 'Fulfill'
the Hebrew Messianic Promises?" <u>The Jewish Spec-
tator</u> (Winter 1977) 3-7

The turbulence of the 1960s was profoundly disturbing to religious leaders in America who saw new religions and Eastern religions capturing the imaginations and mind of much of America's disaffected youth. In 1967, Dr. Carl Henry of <u>Christianity Today</u> wrote an editorial entitled, "Somehow Let's Get Together." He voiced the opinion that if the Christians of America could launch a great evangelistic campaign they might yet create a Christian America. Eventually, a meeting was arranged by evangelist Billy Graham and Carl Henry with a small group of America's prominent religious leaders. They hoped that their plan, Key 73, would be the most ambitious and successful evangelistic program of the century.

Key 73 was not a great success although it managed to involve over 100 religious groups in a united evangelistic campaign. About 50 denominations participated with a budget of two million dollars. Dr. T.A. Raedeke, the director, outlined a six-point program which included a call to prayer in all the participating churches with a synchronized ringing of church bells and honking of car horns, and the distribution of Luke and Acts from the New Testament. The other four phases involved training lay leaders and sending them into their communities to make door-to-door evangelistic visits. The program began on January 6, 1973, with a nationwide TV presentation called "Faith in Action."

The Jewish community was equally disturbed by the loss of its young people to religions such as Christianity as represented by the Hare Krishnas, the Moonies, and Key 73. Although Rabbi Marc H. Tanenbaum, a leader of the Jewish community, admitted in a memorandum issued by the American Jewish Committee that there was no evidence that this evangelistic activity was specifically directed to Jews, he cited the increased activity by the American Board of Missions to the Jews, and the emergence of Jews for Jesus and the Young Hebrew Christian Alliance.

He also raised the question of anti-Semitism in a
criticism of the Broadway rock musical "Jesus
Christ Superstar," which was about to be made
into a film. As a result, the Union of American
Hebrew Congregations published "A Study Kit on
the Film" by Rabbi Balfour Brickner. Yet neither
Jesus Christ Superstar nor Key 73 brought about
any mass conversion of Jews, though a great deal
of polemical material was produced from both the
Jewish and Christian camps.

Handbooks, Brochures, Broadsides and Statements
(by Key 73 and its opposition).

1508. Bichet, Zenas J., ed. "Key 73, Evangelism
Handbook" manuscript, Xeroxed. n.d. 113 pp.

1509. Brickner, Balfour. <u>"Jesus Christ
Superstar," A Study Kit on the Film</u>. New York:
Union of American Hebrew Congregations, 1973. 17
pp.

1510. <u>Jewish Students and the Jesus Movement</u>.
Washington, D.C.: B'nai·B'rith Hillel Foundation,
n.d. (Mimeographed)

1511. <u>Key 73: Calling Our Continent to Christ</u>.
St. Louis, MO: Key 73, n.d.

1512. <u>Key 73: Program Resources</u>. Key 73, n.d. 48
pp.

1513. <u>Launching a Movement</u>. Nashville, TN: Key
73, 6 pp. n.d.

1514. <u>Statement on 'Jesus Christ, Superstar'</u> New
York: National Jewish Community Relations Ad-
visory Council, June 22, 1973.

1515. Syme, D. <u>Know How To Answer - 'Pharisees.'</u>
New York: Union of American Hebrew
Congregations, 1973. 4 pp.

1516. <u>Touched by Fire</u>. 3rd ed. New York:
American Bible Society, 1971. 166 pp.

Magazines and Newspapers

1517. Baum, Gregory. "The Jews, Faith and Ideology." The Ecumenist (July-August 1972) 71-76.

1518. Benjamin, Paul. "'The Key' to Key 73." The Lookout 20 (February 1972) 3-15.

1519. Bernards, Solomon S. "Key 73--A Jewish View." Christian Century (January 3, 1973) 12-14.

1520. Bowler, Maurice G. "Do Jews Need Jesus?" Christianity Today (October 26, 1973) 80-82.

1521. Boyd, Malcolm. "Jesus, Betrayed Again." Ideas (July 15, 1973) 3.

1522. "Christian Evangelism Blasted." Texas Methodist (December 22, 1972).

1523. Doyle, Barrie. "Jewish Furor Over Key 73." Christianity Today (December 22, 1972) 321-322.

1524. "Expo 72 and Key 73 Arousing Suspicions of Jewish Leaders." Street'N Steeple 2 (1972) 2.

1525. Feuerstein, Phyllis. "Describes Conversion Drive Aimed at Some Jews." The Star (February 1, 1972).

1526. "Group Denies Key 73 is Targeted at Jews." Los Angeles Times (February 10, 1973) 26.

1527. Henry, Carl F.H. "Jews Find the Messiah." Christianity Today (April 13, 1973) 28-29.

1528. "Is Jewish Evangelism 'Kosher'?'" Eternity (April 1973) 12-14.

1529. "It Looks as Though Our Jewish Friends are Giving Key 73 the Lift-Off Thrust." The New York Baptist (February 15, 1973) 2.

1530. "Jewish Agency Cites Pros, Cons of Key 73 Ministry." United Methodist Reporter (November 9, 1973).

1531. "Jewish, Christian Theologians Discuss 'Civil Religion.'" The Maryland Baptist (November 23, 1972) 12.

1532. "Jewish Criticism of Key 73 Answered." Western Recorder (March 3, 1973) 6.

1533. "Jews and Jesus." Newsweek (March 19, 1973) 59.

1534. "Jews Evangelizing Jews." Christianity Today (April 23, 1971) 708.

1535. "Jews See Good, Bad in Key 73." Western Recorder (November 3, 1973) 16.

1536. "Jews Taking Hard Line Against Conversion Talk." The Catholic Herald (1973) 2.

1537. "Key 73 Head Responds to Jews." The Texas Methodist 26 (January 1973).

1538. "Key 73 Inertia Cited by Pastor, Rabbi on Panel." United Methodist Register (May 18, 1973).

1539. "Key 73 Negates Jews' Relationship to God, Rabbi Says." Western Recorder (April 7, 1973) 11.

1540. "Key 73 Originator Denounces 'Wolf Cries' Against Evangelism." The Texas Methodist (April 20, 1973).

1541. "Nature of Evangelism is Key 73 Problem – Tanenbaum." Western Recorder (April 7, 1973) 11.

1542. Osburn, Robert T. "A Christian Mission to the Jews?" The Christian Century (November 28, 1973) 1168-1171.

1543. Perlman, Susan. "Furor Over Jewish Evangelism." Eternity (April 1973) 20-23, 47.

1544. "Rabbi Charges that Key 73 'Validates' Radical Groups." The United Methodist Reporter

(March 23, 1973) 3.

1545. "Rabbi Sees Key 73 as Challenge to Judaism." <u>The United Methodist Reporter</u> (August 24, 1973.

1546. "Rabbi Tanenbaum Pleased by Graham Statement on Key 73." <u>Texas Methodist</u> (March 16, 1973).

1547. Ruether, Rosemary. "Theological Anti-Semitism in the New Testament." <u>The Christian Century</u> (February 14, 1968) 191-196.

C. Jewish-Evangelical Dialogue

The dialogue between the Jewish and Liberal Protestant communities and among Jews and Roman Catholics has continued through the twentieth century, only to increase as the horrors of Nazi extermination efforts have become generally known. As a whole, evangelicals (apart from those who remain in the larger denominations) did not participate in such dialogical efforts until the 1970s, to a large extent in response to the Jewish reaction to Key 73. Prior to that time, evangelicals tried to answer the charges of anti-Semitism raised in the landmark sociological study by Charles Y. Glock and Rodney Stark, <u>Christian Beliefs and Anti-Semitism</u> (New York: Harper & Brothers, 1966). Articles in the prominent evangelical magazines, <u>Eternity</u> and <u>Christianity Today</u>, attempted to deal with the issues raised in that volume.

The dialogue begun anew in the mid-1970s has been tentative. To date it has produced few tangible results beyond a self-examination by Evangelicals concerning elements of possible anti-Semitism in traditional evangelical affirmations, but is continuing. The volume by Tanenbaum, Wilson and Rudin (1555) is the product of initial encounters.

Evangelicals share a common concern with the

Jewish community--the state of Israel. This issue
unites them, as evangelicals have generally supported Israel through the political arena. Israel
has become the focus of Jewish attention to evangelical spokespersons such as Jerry Falwell. The
two communities differ radically on evangelism.
Jewish leaders staunchly oppose any efforts at
converting Jews; some consider such activity
anti-Semitic in its very essence.   Evangelicals
consider evangelism to be the essence of their
religious task, and the same theology which leads
them to support Israel so strongly, provides
motivation for targeting Jews for missionary
activity.

1548. Bromley, Geoffrey W. "Who Says the New Testament is Anti-Semitic?" <u>Christianity Today</u>
(March 3, 1967) 12-13.

1549. Carlson, Paul R. <u>O Christian! O Jew!</u> Elgin,
IL: David C. Cook Publishing House, 1974.

1550. Gitlin, Emmanuel. "We Christians Are Your
Agents." <u>Eternity</u> (April 1967) 25, 40.

1551. Maier, Paul L. "Who Was Responsible for the
Trial and Death of Jesus?"   <u>Christianity Today</u>
(April 12, 1974) 8-11.

1552. Menkus, Belden. "Our Subtle Anti-Semitism."
<u>Eternity</u> (April 1967) 23-25.

1553. "The New Testament and the Jew." <u>Chris-
tianity Today</u> (June 7, 1968) 22-23.

1554. Simon, Merrill. <u>Jerry Falwell and the Jews</u>.
Middle Village, NY: Jonathan David Publishers,
1984. 172pp.

1555. Tanenbaum, Marc H., Marvin R. Wilson amd A.
James Rudin. <u>Evangelicals and Jews in Conversa-
tion on Scripture, Theology, and History</u>. Grand
Rapids, MI: Baker Book House, 1978. 326pp.

1556. -----. <u>Evangelicals and Jews in an Age of
Pluralism</u>. Grand Rapids, MI: Baker Book House,
1984. 285pp.

1557. Waldorf, Frank M. "How Jews Look at Love and Marriage." _Eternity_ (April 1967) 26, 46-7.

1558. Wilson, Marvin R. "An Evangelical Perspective on Judaism." _Evangelical Theological Society Journal_ 19:3 (Summer 1976) 169-90.

1559. Young, G. Douglas. "Lessons We Can Learn from Judaism." _Eternity_ (April 1967) 22.

D. Sholem Asch (1880-1951)

The missionary activity of Christian and Jewish Christian groups was a burden accepted by Jewish groups in the first half of the 20th century. Judaism flourished and the missionary societies, including the American Board of Missions to the Jews, made little progress. Yet Jews in the U.S., like the gentile immigrants, shed their Old World ways, trading Yiddish for English and European customs for new American ones. Religious orthodoxy, in particular, had a difficult struggle against Americanization; if few Jews were lost through missionary activities, many were lost through intermarriage and assimilation. Hence, the Jewish community reacted strongly when their foremost writer, Sholem Asch, produced a trilogy of books with a Christian theme. His novel about the life of Christ, _The Nazarene_, appeared in 1939 and was an instant best seller; it was followed by _The Apostle_ in 1943 and _Mary_ in 1949. The fact that a member of the Jewish community wrote best sellers with Christian themes was regarded by many Jews as a betrayal.

Chaim Lieberman, a columnist for the _Jewish Daily Forward_, published an extremely antagonistic book, _The Christianity of Sholem Asch_. Not alone in his condemnation of Asch, Lieberman charged him with anti-Semitism. _The Jewish Daily Forward_ stopped publishing his material and he was pressured into dropping out of the Jewish Agency for Palestine. Two years after the publication of <u>The Nazarene</u>, Asch published a personal statement of faith entitled <u>What I Believe</u>. He claimed that his research and writing of <u>The Nazarene</u> served to strengthen his Judaism and he reaffirmed his intention to improve Jewish/Christian understanding. He felt that because Jesus was the best known and most influential Jew of all time, his life should be interpreted by a fellow Jew. Yet neither Jews nor Christians could understand how a Jew could write such books without professing Christianity.

Asch died in Israel in 1951, remaining an enigma to both Jews and gentiles. He accomplished little in his attempt to bridge the gap between Jews and Christians, although he reminded the world that Jesus was a Jew and that Christian roots were in Judaism. His work may well have prepared the ground for the emergence of the Messianic movement of the 1960s in which the Jews for Jesus and others embraced Christianity while maintaining their Jewish culture and some of their Jewish religious practices.

1560. Asch, Sholem. <u>The Apostle</u>. Translated by Maurice Samuel. New York: G.P. Putnam's Sons, 1943. 745pp.

1561. ------. <u>East River</u>. Translated by A.H. Gross. New York: G.P. Putnam's Sons, 1946. 438pp.

1562. ------. <u>The Mother</u>. Translated by Elsa Krauch. Garden City, NY: The Sun Dial Press, 1937. 295pp.

1563. ------. <u>The Nazarene</u>. Translated by Maurice Samuel. New York: G.P. Putnam's Sons, 1939. 698pp.

1564. ------. <u>One Destiny</u>. New York: G.P. Putnam's Sons, 1945. 88pp.

1565. ------. <u>A Passage in the Night</u>. New York: G.P. Putnam's Sons. 1953. 367pp.

1566. ------. <u>The Prophet</u>. Translated by Arthur Saul Super. New York: G.P. Putnam's Sons, 1955.

343pp.

1567. -----. "What I Believe." Translated by
Maurice Samuel, New York: G.P. Putnam's Sons,
1941. 201pp.

1568. Lieberman, Chaim. The Christianity of
Sholem Asch. New York: Philosophical Library,
1953. 276pp.

SECTION SEVEN

JEWISH CHRISTIANITY-WHAT DIRECTION WILL IT
TAKE?

The story of Jewish Christianity is an old one: if we believe a writer like Hugh J. Schonfield, its history is simultaneous with that of Christianity; but if we believe Jewish critics, it has never existed. This writer holds the view that people have the right to choose the name that they feel best expresses their identity. Over the years, Christians have chosen to call themselves: Jews, Hebrew Christians, and Messianists. This book has been about all of these and the critics who would deny them.

In reading the history of these groups, one sees that by the 5th century after Christ, few distinctly Jewish Christian communities existed. Gentile Christians, who had outnumbered their Jewish brethren since the first century after Christ, feared that separate Jewish Christian congregations would harbor the heresy of "Judaizing." Thus, Jews who responded to the gospel became members of gentile congregations and, in time, were assimilated. Over the next 1,200 years, the distinction between Jew and Gentile disappeared within the Christian church. The Protestant Reformation of the 16th century sparked the reemergence of distinctly Jewish Christian congregations. Thomas Brightman, in _Apocalypis Apocalypseos_, called for Jewish restoration to the Holy Land which not only marked the beginning of Zionism, but revived in Jewish Christians a sense of pride in their Jewish heritage. During the missionary movement of the 18th and 19th centuries, converted Jews began to refer to themselves as Hebrew Christians. But again the fears regarding Judaizing were raised and the debate continued into the 20th century. Some Hebrew Christian congregations appeared in the late 19th and early 20th centuries in Europe and the U.S. although the majority of Jewish believers joined gentile churches and became assimilated into gentile society.

The 1960s brought a new emergence of Jewish Christianity. In the U.S. today, there are over 100 congregations which preach the gospel of Jesus Christ while preserving the Jewish cultural heritage. Although the growth rate has decreased since the 1960s, there is no indication that the number of Jewish converts per year is declining. Yet Jews have been, in many ways, like immigrants; as the various groups have become "Americanized," the old neighborhoods have broken up and the younger generations have lost their languages and cultures. Several centuries of discrimination against Jews, specifically, have resulted in separate Jewish and gentile cultural patterns. Subsequently many Jews do not feel at home, and in some cases not welcome, in many gentile congregations. Yet there have always been Christians who were gentiles and Christians who were Jews. The Messianic congregations that have appeared since the 1960s are trying to influence the gentile community to accept the idea of Jewish Christianity. It is significant that a number of new books by Jewish critics refer to "Jewish Christianity." Though the title appears in quotation marks, it signifies some recognition.

Whether distinctive Jewish Christian congregations survive or not will depend, in part, on how successfully present congregations establish that it is possible for a Jew to be a Christian. If the concept is accepted, Jews will no longer feel the need of a distinctly Jewish congregation. In addition, intermar-

riage is increasing and in more cases than not,
the Jewish community loses members to Christian
churches.   Furthermore,   and   somewhat
ironically,   new   attitudes   in   the   major
denominations and in some fundamentalist groups
are leading to more conversions.

On the other hand, many in the Jewish community are fearful of Christian evangelism and
consequently   there   is   a   flood   of   literature
addressed   to   both   the   Jewish   and   gentile
communities.   Books   such   as   <u>Jews and "Jewish
Christianity"</u>   by   David   Berger   and   Michael
Wyschogrod   are   written   primarily   for   Jews   who
have been attracted by Jews for Jesus and other
Christian   evangelistic   groups.   They   present
arguments   as   to   why   Jews   should   not   become
Christians, though saying that it is all right
for gentiles to do so.

Unless there is a revival of Judaism or a
revival of intolerance, Jews will probably continue to become members of the Christian community in the U.S. in increasing numbers.   Although the American melting pot has tended to
break down ethnic barriers, causing Americans
to identify themselves as Protestant, Catholic,
or Jew, only Jews in large urban areas can
easily find Jewish congregations.   In rural
areas and small towns that do not have Jewish
congregations, Jews will continue to find themselves drawn to the dominant religious groups
if there are no barriers of discrimination or
culture. At present, there are about 20,000 to
30,000 Jewish Christians, half of which are in
distinctive Jewish congregations.   I believe
that this number will increase slightly over
the next three or four decades but also that
all religions will represent a smaller percentage of the national population than at present.

Finally, I believe that distinctly Jewish
congregations will disappear within two or
three generations as the descendants of the
present congregations find their way into main
stream denominations.   I also believe that
Jewish Christians will become a recognized
force within the American church, and their

presence will make Christians more aware of
their Jewish heritage. Relations between Jews
and gentiles may or may not improve, but the
church will be stronger for having rediscovered
its roots.

Index of Authors

Kimball, Earl H. 483
Kirban, Salem 60-61
Klein, Charlotte 256
Klijn, A.F. 26
Klingeman, Aaron Judah 1418-24
Klyber, Arthur B. 200-203
Koenig, Jeffrey 1239-41
Kopp, E. Paul 1053-55
Korotkin, Shelley 1242-43
Kosmala, Hans 334
Kostroff, Mike 1244
Kreider, Roy 1109
Kress, Vickie 1245-48
Kripke, Myer S. 1493
Kroll, Woodrow M. 652
Kroupa, Carol 1249
Kugler, Irving D. 1250
Kurkowske, Adolph 285
Kutner, John 1110

L
Lagona, James F. 1111
LaHaye, Tim 62
LaMagdeleine, Donald R. 1368
Lambert, Lance 63
Lapids, Pinchas E. 204
Lascelle, Ruth Specter 971-73, 990-1021
Lasker, Daniel J. 1494
Lasky, William R. 1112
Lee, Robert G. 1113
Le-Israel, Eduth 1022
Leverhoff, Paul 1114
Levine, Dan 1251
Levine, Samuel 1495
Levitt, Zola 65, 72, 73, 370, 379-98, 400-05,
408-12
Levy, Asher 901
Levy, David M. 711
Levy, Mark John 1441-45
Levy, Rosalie Marie 205-18
Lew, Ben David 857-63
Lew, Esther 863
Lewis, David Allen 88-89
Lieberman, Chaim1425, 1568
Lightle, Steve 63
Lindberg, Milton B. 534-42, 556-60
Lindsey, Hal 66-71
Linton, John 653

Richardson, Peter 32
Richman, Kresha 1280
Robert, Brother 222
Robinson, Rich 1281-82
Roddy, Lee 961
Rogers, W.H. 500-02
Rohold, S.R. 1428
Rosen, Ceil 397, 1154, 1283-86
Rosen, Martin 1155-56, 1372
Rosen, Moishe 1154-60, 1287-1331, 1372-75
Rosen, Ruth 1332-34
Rosenberg, Leon I. 519-25
Rosenblum, Larry 1335
Rosenthal, Jacob 1029
Rosenthal, Marvin J. 714-19
Rosenthal, Stanley 720
Roth, Sid 1462
Rothchild, Walter 138, 1128
Roy, Kristina1129
Rubin, Barry 1336
Rubin, Reuben 1337
Rubin, Steffi 1161, 1338-39
Rudin, A. James 1501, 1555-56
Rudin, Marcia 1501
Rudolph, George 1130
Ruether, Rosemary 1547
Rutherford, Joseph Franklin 100

S
Sandmel, Samuel 33
Sacks, Herschel 1340
Sacks, Wendy 1341
Saxe, Israel 563
Schaeffer, Edith 1132
Schiffman, Robyn 1342
Schlamm, Vera 281, 1162
Schlissel, Steve 504
Schneider, Abraham 872
Schneider, Peter 343
Schonfield, Hugh J. 34
Schor, Samuel 81
Schriebman, Elinor 1343-44
Schwartz, Steve 407
Scott, Delaware W. 335
Shank, Robert 82
Shapiro, B. A. M. 747-74
Sharif, Regina 83
Sherman, Shlomah 1502